REDESIGN

An SEL Toolkit to Designing
Culturally Sustaining and Antiracist Practices

Dwayne D. Williams

"The murder of George Floyd has challenged Americans to look in the mirror. What they see is rampant systemic racism, whether it's in the boardroom, in the classroom or in the courtroom. Brother Williams's *Redesign* is the educational resource needed to thoughtfully navigate renegotiating how administrators and teachers can do right by students of color. The project's focus on using SEL practices to heal the achievement gap's 'wound of inequity' is needed now more than ever. Allow *Redesign* to guide you on this journey."

~**Michael M. Smith**, Assistant Principal
Township High School District 211

"Dwayne D. Williams illustrates how trauma associated with the Black American experience derives from a systemic tradition of anti-Blackness. The impact of this trauma on the teaching and learning for students and educators of color necessitates the redesigning of educational practices grounded in social emotional learning. If educational institutions and individual practitioners are authentic in the call for antiracism, *Redesign* positions organizations to do the adaptive and technical work that leads to equitable student outcomes."

~**LeVar J. Ammons, Ed.D**, Executive Director of Equity and Student Success
Oak Park and River Forest High School

"*Redesign* is a necessary resource for all teachers, whether new to the profession or experienced in the classroom. As a teacher, I crave opportunities to serve all my students better. As a White teacher, I need to reflect on my own thoughts and understandings of race and culture by using the theoretical frameworks and best practices in *Redesign's* activity section."

~**Sue Howard**, Teacher
Hinsdale Township High School District 86

"Dwayne D. Williams has filled a gap within the literature by providing practitioners with a toolkit to deeply examine our own experiences with race as a first step to addressing and developing antiracist programming and culturally sustaining practices. As practitioners at the ground level doing the work, we need this toolkit now more than ever. This book is an essential read for school-based professionals who desire to establish practices that are culturally sustaining and antiracist."

~**Miguel Salinas**, Certified Bilingual School Psychologist
CEO of Salinas Educational Services

"Fortunately for educators and stakeholders, Dwayne's work outlines succinct measures in ensuring educational environments where culturally and linguistically diverse learners can be seen and supported from a strengths-based approach. This is the exact disposition that is necessary in combating anti-Black racism. This timely and timeless body of work will translate into improved educational attainment for students from underserved communities. This is the moment."

~**April Wells**, Gifted Coordinator and author of the book *Achieving Equity in Gifted Programming: Dismantling Barriers and Tapping Potential*
School District U-46

"I too am tired. As an educator who has worked with Black and Brown students for over two decades—mostly under federal consent decrees because we continue to fail our children—I applaud Dwayne D. Williams for writing a book that is long overdue. *Redesign* is amazing, practical, and written by a fellow colleague who remains in the trenches doing the work. Much needed and appreciated!"

~**Dr. Tiffany Gholson**, LCSW, Director of Parent and Student Support Services
East Saint Louis School District #189

"We educators cannot control what happens in the homes of our students, but we can certainly strive to educate inside and outside the classroom for the betterment of our human experience. I had been a colleague of Dwayne's for more than 5 years, and I can say that he had expressed the concerns of race and culture that *Redesign* addresses the day we met, and he challenged our problem-solving teams to reconsider our own practices. His ability to write and train on issues of race, culture, and equity without judgment speaks to his value in this new world where a silent enemy, racism, is hurting *all* people. This silence—the challenge of speaking on issues of race, equity, and justice—only strengthens our enemy. If you desire to break the silence in your homes and schools by rejecting and resisting racist practices and policies, and to prepare your children and students to become antiracist citizens, I encourage you to start with this book."

~**Jennifer Reyes**, Assistant Principal of Student Services,
East Aurora High School

Redesigning Discipline Practices and Policies

by
Dr. Robin Vannoy,
Director of Deans
Hinsdale South High School

I felt a wave of emotion come over me. I could not control the tears that were falling from my face. I was at a racial equity workshop for educators. The facilitator challenged us to acknowledge the harm we had caused Black students in general and Black males in particular. He argued that we operate within an educational system that regularly causes harm to Black students. Some would argue that it is designed to keep Black students from succeeding.

I took a deep breath and allowed myself to feel the ways I had hurt Black students.

When I hurt them, I did not think about the pain I caused or how I affected them socially and emotionally. When I hurt them, I followed directives: I followed our school's protocol. I was a dean, and it was my job to maintain the safety and security of the school. If students engaged in a physical altercation, it was my job to punish them, which usually ended in external suspensions. This was our school's policy and expectation.

It seemed that no one thought of the detrimental impact our policies and practices had on students of color. I surely did not. As I reflected on my experiences in my seat at the conference, my body became warm, and I immediately scanned the room to see how other educators were experiencing the moment, for I certainly could not have been the only one in the room who enacted policies that were detrimental to the achievement of Black students. Following the workshop, a number of questions swirled through my mind. As educators, do we acknowledge the ways we hurt students? Are we aware? Do we care? What actions do we take after we realize we have caused harm to ensure that it never happens again? We must take an honest look at ourselves and examine our actions. No more excuses. We must then focus on redesigning our practices and policies in ways that are inclusive and equitable for all students, including students who have been historically marginalized because of oppressive beliefs and ideologies. One way of doing this is by concentrating on what is within our sphere of control and by transforming the spaces that we occupy into learning environments that promote the achievement of all students, not just some students. As an African American woman in charge of discipline, I am committed to protecting the hearts, bodies, and minds of all students. This can be done by redesigning antiquated disciplinary practices and policies into antiracist and equitable practices and policies.

Redesigning Writing Workshop by Incorporating Culturally Meaningful *Proactive Circles*

by
Sue Howard, Teacher
Hinsdale South High School

In our 2019 Writing Workshop course, my co-teacher and I found ourselves focused on behavior and not the disparate, academic needs of our students. While observing students concerned about their phones, leaving class, or expecting us to individually repeat directions, we became disheartened. This course typically includes a high number of students with IEPs, along with a disproportionate number of Black and Brown students. Originally, I believed my determination and loving intentions could provide a fulfilling experience for each student, but I soon realized these small behavioral challenges indicated a larger institutional disconnect between educators and students.

After speaking with our Director of Deans and Special Education Chair, I was surprised to see that instead of specific issues or students, we talked about a process which could help: proactive circles. Traditionally intended to provide participants with a safe space to air concerns, we wanted to also add a level of community, encouraging participants to share intimate stories and to sympathize across differences.

Similar to Dwayne D. Williams' *Redesign* activities, the conversations we had with Dwayne and our Student Support Coordinator started with reflective questions. My original goal of curbing cell phone use soon took a back seat as the interventionists directed me to think more globally and with intention. Although an experienced teacher, I needed to reflect on what misunderstandings I have about race and students with different experiences than my own.

As a middle-aged White woman, my experiences are not similar to many of my students' experiences. For instance, if one of my daughters had an emergency while away at college, I could immediately leave work and go to her. While I understand not all families have this privilege—a secure job and means to travel—I learned that my bias must go beyond the lens of my former experiences. I must not only recognize differences, but apply that recognition to the forefront of my teaching.

I need to listen better and ask for assistance in understanding my students. After complimenting the class for good behavior, one of my students said, "Ms. Howard, I'm going to give you some Black people lessons. We don't like to be complimented—it makes us feel weak." I smiled and assumed he was joking, but have since come to understand what he actually meant was that kids don't like it when adults have a lack of confidence in them. By complimenting his good behavior, it sent the message that I was surprised that he could behave. I felt crushed because I did not recognize what he was telling me in the moment; it was a missed opportunity to connect with a student. I cannot teach from my White perspective and assume non-white students will benefit equitably.

As our students got stronger in sharing and holding each other accountable, those who were reluctant to talk earlier in the semester eventually opened up. We moved from the interventionists to the teachers to eventually the students leading circles, and our student attendance improved. Engagement cannot be forced. It is rooted in an authentic understanding and respect. Students shared feelings about Kobe Bryant's death and *Hair Love* winning the Oscar for Best Short Film, in addition to personal experiences told through music and spoken word. Proactive circles provided us with a way to learn our students' stories, and most importantly, they informed our instruction to lend a guiding hand as our students take responsibility and power over their own educational journey.

As a novice with proactive circles, I will have many eye-opening and transformative lessons in my future. Working directly with Dwayne D. Williams, author of *Redesign*, I was able to redesign my approach to how I looked for solutions in the classroom. For those not fortunate to have Dwayne as a trusted colleague, this text will take you through a similar process as though he is walking along with you. My hope, as a teacher, is that my students can advocate for their personal identities. My role as a teacher is to be racially and culturally aware enough to provide the space, time and comfort to do so.

REDESIGN:

to revise in appearance, function, or content
-Merriam Webster Dictionary Online

Cover design, text pages and layout: Dan Yeager, Nu-Image Design; Editor: Geoff Fuller

Other books by Dwayne D. Williams:

Like Music to My Ears: A Hip-Hop Approach to SEL and Trauma in Schools
ISBN: 978-0-9847157-5-6

An RTI Guide to Improving the Performance of African American Students
ISBN: 978-1483319735

Human Behavior from a Spiritual Perspective: Spiritual Development Begins in Your Mind
Book 1: ISBN: 978-0984715794
Book 2: ISBN: 978-0984715787

Visit Begin With Their Culture Bookstore to View Additional Resources at the Website Below
Contact Dwayne D. Williams at:
Email: dwayne@tier1education.com
Website: www.tier1education.com
Twitter: @dwaynedwilliams
Redesign Private Facebook Group: https://www.facebook.com/groups/redesignAnseltoolkit
Facebook: www.facebook.com/Tier1services
LinkedIn: https://www.linkedin.com/in/dwayne-d-williams-71212b39/
Instagram: beginwiththeirculture
YouTube Channel: https://www.youtube.com/channel/UCm9a3oNeIN_R_kxleU_XQOQ

ACKNOWLEDGMENTS

I am indebted to my educator colleagues who provided suggestions, feedback, and recommendations for this work. Specifically, I would like to thank Geoff Fuller, Dan Yeager, Sue Howard, Michael M. Smith, Dr. Robin Vannoy, Stephen Moore, Megan Parker, April Wells, Dianna Palumbo, Jen Gressens House, Denise Gates, Dr. Tiffany Gholson, Dr. LeVar Ammons, Miguel Salinas, Jennifer Reyes, and Adam Page. Thank you for the part you played in the design of this book.

Shoutout to all my educator brothers and sisters who are currently seeking to create culturally sustaining, inclusive, and antiracist practices. No matter your race, color, or background, I am your brother in the field. I am at the ground level with you in this work, striving to improve the wellbeing of all students by providing equitable opportunities and practices in the classroom.

I appreciate you. I am grateful for you. I love you.

In solidarity,
Dwayne D. Williams

ACKNOWLEDGMENT

Contents

Redesigning Discipline Practices and Policies   7
Redesigning Writing Workshop by Incorporating
Culturally Meaningful Proactive Circles   9
Acknowledgments   13
About the Author   17
Keywords   19

Introduction: Racial Trauma   **21**
Redesign Overview   23
The Brown Paper Bag Experience   24
SEL and Reflective Activities   26

Chapter 1: Antiracist Education   **29**
What Are You Teaching for and What Are You Teaching Against?   31
Antiracist Education and Culturally Sustaining Practices   32
What's in the Name "Antiracist Education?"   33

Chapter 2: Reflection   **35**
My Journey   36
Antiracist Education, Practices, and Policies   39

Chapter 3: The Framework   **41**
Cultural Historical Activity Theory   43
Cultural   44
Historical   45
Activity   45
Theory   47
Culturally Sustaining Pedagogy   47
Social Emotional Learning and the Toolkit   48
Redesign Facebook Online Community of Practice   50

Chapter 4: SEL Activities and Racial History   **53**
I. Self-Awareness Activities   **57**
Activity 1.1: Your Racial-Cultural Journey Map   58
Activity 1.2: Reflection   63
Activity 1.3: Teacher Training Programs   69
Activity 1.4: Current Practices   72

II. Social-Awareness Activities   **76**
Activity 2.1: Engagement Among Students of Color   77
Activity 2.2: Student Perception of Racially Explicit Content   81

III. Self-Management Activities   **84**
Activity 3.1: Activist Burnout   85
Activity 3.2: Designing Your Self-Care Plan   88
Activity 3.3: Racial Trauma   98

IV. Relationship Skills Activities   **102**
Activity 4.1: Relationship Directory   103

V. Responsible Decision-Making Activities   **106**
Activity 5.1: Resolving Current Challenges   107

Next Step?   **112**
Terms to Know When Considering Educational Equity Work   **114**
References   **118**

ABOUT THE AUTHOR

Dwayne D. Williams is a school psychologist, interventionist, and educational consultant. As a consultant, Dwayne helps organizations design and redesign educational practices. Specifically, he helps teams create culturally sustaining, inclusive, and equitable programming that mixes instruction with the cultural assets and lived experiences of students. Additionally, Dwayne provides training to school districts on how to design problem-solving models, multitiered systems of support, restorative practices, social emotional learning, and trauma-informed groups—all from a culturally sustaining lens.

Dwayne is the CEO of *Tier 1 Educational Coaching and Consulting Firm*, an organization that helps districts redesign educational practices in ways that pair issues of race, culture, and equity with instruction. He is the author of the book *An RTI Guide to Improving Performance of African American Students.* He has used his curriculum, *Like Music to My Ears: A Hip-Hop Approach to Addressing Social Emotional Learning and Trauma in Schools*, with hundreds of students, and he coaches practitioners through the process of designing activities that integrate SEL, cognitive behavioral therapeutic practices, and hip-hop cultural elements as methods of employing culturally sustaining practices for students who embrace the arts.

Dwayne is currently a PhD student at the University of Illinois at Chicago, where he studies curriculum and instruction. His scholarship focuses on redesigning educational programming in ways that consider the cultural assets and lived experiences of culturally diverse learners. Dwayne lived in housing projects as a child, in Springfield, Illinois, and often speaks on the need to connect with students, parents, and community leaders from underrepresented backgrounds in order to improve educational conditions for underrepresented groups.

Dwayne is married to Toni Williams, and together they have two children: Dwayne D. Williams II and Noni D. Williams.

Keywords:

antiracist education
cultural historical activity theory (CHAT)
culturally relevant/responsive teaching
culturally sustaining pedagogy (CSP)
equity
inclusive
racial trauma
redesign
relationship skills
responsible decision-making
self-awareness
self-management
social awareness
social emotional learning

Introduction: Racial Trauma

"I can't breathe."
~ Eric Garner ~ Javier Ambler II ~ Manny Ellis ~ George Floyd . . .

On July 2, 2020, a colleague and friend of mine asked me why I had been silent on social media concerning the deaths of Ahmaud Arbery, Breonna Taylor, and George Floyd, and why I had not expressed concern regarding racial injustice, including the inhumane treatment of Black and Brown people by government officials. My colleague was spot on. I was silent. I was avoidant. I was absent. She was not the only person to identify my inaction. Others did as well. But what she and others did not see was my hurt. My pain. My frustration. I did not want to deal with the reality of Brother George calling for his mother and begging for his life, stating that he could not breathe over twenty times, while an officer knelt on his neck for eight minutes and forty-six seconds. I did not want to talk about that at the moment. I did not want to process it. When I came across the story on CNN and other news outlets, I quickly turned the television off. I didn't want to think about Brother George's reality—or the reality of Brother Ahmaud, who was hunted down by two White men while peacefully jogging, or Sister Breonna, who was killed by police invading her home.

Yes. I was silent. I was avoidant. I was absent.

My response to the events reminds me of how one of my students responded to traumatic events that affected him socially, emotionally, spiritually, and physically. While helping him process trauma and talk about his experiences, I encouraged him to create a journey map, a map of his life leading up to the traumatic events. The goal was to re-expose my student to the trauma he experienced by guiding him as he drew images of his memories, helping him process thoughts and emotions that emerged from the experience, while teaching breathing techniques throughout the process. I employed exposure therapeutic strategies to help him process traumatic events.

My student eagerly grabbed a sheet of art paper and began illustrating his journey. As he recalled his experiences, he wrote a word on his map; the word was "tired."

"Hmm," I said. "This word is powerful. It quickly caught my eye." I lifted the map from my desk and brought it closer to my face. I was not wearing my glasses and could barely see the details of his work. "What do you mean by tired? What does this mean?"

"Aw, Mr. Williams, it's like . . . it's like . . . you feel me . . . it's like. . . ." He slowly looked in the air and around my office as he tried to find the most appropriate way to describe his thoughts concerning the word *tired* and how it related to his life. He eventually responded: "It's like, I'm just tired. That's it. There is no other way of saying it. I try to avoid it. I don't like talking about it. It's so hard!"

He continued, "I have been through all of this." He pointed to the events on his map as he spoke. "And so I'm just tired. I'm tired of dealing with it. I'm tired of thoughts that enter my mind. I'm tired of crying about it. I'm just tired."

As my student expressed his feelings, he became emotional. His hands flailed the air wildly. It was evident by his behaviors and emotions that he was tired, that he was frustrated, that he was fed up. I helped my student process traumatic events that disrupted his life and taught him self-management techniques to deal with his pain.

Tired. Frustrated. Fed up. I am tired. I am frustrated. I am fed up. The words of my student accurately describe how I experienced the events of my brothers George and Ahmaud and my sister Breonna. My student's response is common to many people who deal with the stress of traumatic events, especially when the trauma occurs again and again and again. While my student's experiences and my experiences were different, we both experienced events that triggered physiological and psychological stress responses in our bodies and minds. The reality is that we all have or will have to deal with traumatic events, and we will respond to these events in various ways. When I experience racial trauma, I become silent and reflective. I recall racialized events that occurred in my life, events that I witnessed indirectly in my own communities and events that I experienced directly and personally. As a school psychologist and interventionist who works with students of color, and as a father with Black children of my own, my mind shifts to the question, What do students of color need to know and be able to do in order to act as agents when experiencing discrimination, injustice, and oppressive events in society? My mind shifts to my White brothers and sisters in education, my White allies. What do they need to know and be able to do in order to prepare Black and Brown students to act as agents when facing discrimination, racism, and injustice? My thoughts, my silence, my avoidance, my experiences compelled me to write this book, and my hope is that it will generate dialogue and action around inclusive and antiracist practices.

Redesign Overview

There is no doubt that educational policies and practices require an overhaul, a redo, a redesign. While this is true, important questions are, Where should practitioners and organizational leaders start when redesigning policies and classroom-based practices in order to ensure equitable and inclusive programming for all students? What are your thoughts? What do you say? Where do we start? Take a moment to reflect on these questions, as they are critical because our starting point will dictate subsequent actions in the redesign process. If leaders start with the wrong approach, they will find it difficult at best to get practitioners to retrace their steps, to rethink their actions, to redesign their practices. Therefore, educational leaders must think long and hard about their first step in redesigning policies and practices in their organization and introducing culturally sustaining, inclusive, and antiracist work to teachers.

While there are many places to start when considering the redesign of educational policies and practices, my argument in this book is that we start with our lived experiences with race and culture. I argue that we start with ourselves: with our attitudes, beliefs, and perspectives about race, culture, and racial group members. This approach is distinct from starting with instructional practices and student-based interventions. If we start with instructional practices, it is possible to design culturally meaningful activities that integrate the cultural assets and lived experiences of students of color, yet maintain racist mindsets, attitudes, and beliefs about their heritages, languages, literacies, identities, and ways of being. The tendency to attempt redesign by starting with instructional practices and inserting into agendas and lesson plans something of "cultural relevance" for Black and Brown students is certainly common in education. I cannot express enough how backward this approach is, the practice of providing "culturally meaningful" activities for students of color while maintaining negative perceptions about their being. I have witnessed this phenomenon far too many times; it is disgusting, oppressive, and racist.

Redesigning educational and workplace practices by starting with student-based interventions aligns with deficit-based, racist thinking that supports the contested belief that something is wrong with Black and Brown kids and we must fix them in order to improve their social and educational conditions. With this thinking we absolve ourselves in a way similar to the racist scholars of the 1960s and 1970s, who deemed the cultures, languages, and literacies of people of color inherently inferior to those of the White race. We must start with ourselves, with our own lived experiences with race and culture, and examine how racial and cultural events have shaped our identities as individuals, as racial and cultural group members, and as educators. I argue that we begin by reflecting on racial and cultural experiences in order to examine how these experiences have shaped our attitudes about culturally relevant, responsive, and sustaining teaching. I believe that, rather than starting with instructional practices, we must start with our own personal histories, which we pull from our subconscious, lived experiences and events that have shaped our attitudes and beliefs about race, culture, and equity.

The Brown Paper Bag Experience

Years ago, I facilitated a brown paper-bag luncheon for practitioners and administrators in a district in the Midwest, where we discussed race, social justice, and education. During one of the sessions, practitioners entered the conference room, where we all laughed, acknowledged one another's presence, and prepared for our discussion. We were all in good spirits. During this session, I guided practitioners through the process of reflecting on their lived experiences with race. One of the teachers began to share a story about an event that happened in her young adult life. Her lips quivered, and she took deep breaths in order to get her words out. She began to cry hysterically, unable to share her experience initially. Group members comforted her as she gathered herself and her thoughts, while breathing deeply. When she was able to share her lived experience with race, she talked about an event that took place with a Black male. The experience was traumatizing for her. The teacher shared that she often thinks about the traumatic event. She commented that "taller, big, Black male" students trigger traumatic, intrusive thoughts related to a Black male of her past. She explained that her experience affects how she perceives and responds to males of color.

Another teacher who reflected on her racial history shared that engaging in self-guided activities with race can be challenging. For this reason, I included in this book an activity that works as a tool to help practitioners reflect on their racial and cultural history (see chapter four, Activity 1.1). The activity provides opportunities for practitioners to connect with other racially and culturally diverse people to share and process racial experiences and to examine how those experiences shape our current thinking, attitudes, and behaviors as educators.

For the past decade, I have been training administrators and practitioners on how to design culturally inclusive and equitable practices for culturally diverse learners; the design process focused on rejecting the tendency to automatically apply Eurocentric theories, values, and practices when working with Black and Brown students whose values may clash with Eurocentric systems. Additionally, I have dedicated the past decade to redesigning my own practices to reject the reliance on Eurocentric theories, values, and ways of practicing school psychology. I want a more culturally sustaining, inclusive, and antiracist approach to preparing students to challenge and resist racist policies, practices, and perspectives. In this book, I use practical activities to guide readers through the process of reflecting on their lived experiences with race and culture as a starting point to designing equitable practices. I do this because, as Gay (2018) argues, educators must interrogate their beliefs and attitudes concerning students of color and their abilities when implementing supports, while carefully rejecting theories and perspectives that deem students of color as pathological and backward people.

For this reason, I take readers on a reflective journey of their lived experiences with race and culture in order to examine how racial and cultural experiences over the course of their lives have affected their mindset, attitudes, and beliefs as educators. I use CASEL's (2020) five social emotional learning (SEL) competencies—self-awareness, self-management, social awareness, relationship skills, and responsible decision-making—in culturally meaningful ways and as tools to guide readers through the process of reflecting on lived experiences with race and culture.

SEL and Reflective Activities

Drawing from SEL competencies, critical questions that we must ask ourselves when redesigning educational programming include the following: What racial and cultural events have I experienced that have contributed to my current beliefs, attitudes, and perspectives concerning race, culture, and students of color? How do these beliefs and attitudes influence the ways in which I think about, interact with, and set standards for students of color? Additionally, how do my perspectives, attitudes, and beliefs about students of color make me feel concerning their presence, cultures, literacies, identities, and languages? These questions relate to both *self-awareness* and *social awareness*. They pertain to *self-awareness* in that they reflect on lived experiences with race and culture to bring to our consciousness personal histories regarding race relations that influence our current thinking. They pertain to *social awareness* in that they guide us through the process of scanning, from a personal-historical approach, social events and experiences that shape our current beliefs and attitudes about students of color, their parents, their communities, and their cultures.

We must also ask ourselves questions concerning self-care and identify strategies that will help us calm and manage ourselves when we experience stress, tension, and anxiety as a result of racial-cultural-equity work. Important reflective questions are: How am I caring for myself so that I may care for others when redesigning racist practices? How often do I engage in activities that will help me de-stress and recharge when engaging with this work? Have I constructed a self-care plan, and if so, how often do I follow it? Such questions are critical to redesigning educational practices and are associated with self-management. If we do not think seriously about how we manage and care for ourselves, it is possible that we will burn out, become complacent, and discontinue our efforts at redesign.

Still, we must ask questions of relationship skills and responsible decision-making. In what ways does relationship-building assist in the effective redesign of educational practices? What constitutes responsible decision-making when redesigning educational practices? When redesigning work activity, our success depends on collaborative relationships with allies across race and culture. Connecting with others who are redesigning educational practices provides partners the opportunity to run through ideas and process thoughts and feelings. Regarding responsible decision-making, I argue that educators who desire to redesign their work in ways that lead to antiracist programming must (1) read and process scholarship on the topic of work redesign, (2) interact in redesign groups such as communities of practice, (3) identify theoretical frameworks that will guide educational redesign, and (4) work collaboratively with allies at the ground level to resolve challenges that interfere with redesigning activities. Using SEL competencies to guide the redesign of racist programming and policies requires that we practice what we preach; it requires that we practice the very SEL competencies that we encourage our students to practice while they are in school and out of school. Therefore, this book draws from SEL scholarship (along with other theoretical frameworks that I will discuss in chapter 3) in order to start the process of disrupting racist policies and practices, and redesigning educational activities in ways that not only acknowledge the cultural values and lived experiences of students, but also foster and sustain cultural identities, assets, languages, and literacies.

Redesign will guide you through the process of

- reflecting on lived experiences with race and culture through a personal, historical lens in order to prepare for antiracist and culturally sustaining work;
- identifying how your historical experiences with race and culture influence your current beliefs, attitudes, and practices;
- questioning, critiquing, criticizing, and rejecting racist, oppressive practices;
- identifying and resolving personal challenges that interfere with designing culturally sustaining antiracist programming.

This book is guided by four principles: (1) beliefs and attitudes concerning racial-cultural-equity programming guide educational practices, (2) all five SEL competencies are central to designing culturally sustaining, inclusive, and antiracist programming, (3) redesigning practices in ways that are equitable and inclusive requires a fine balance of theory and practice concerning both *antiracist* education and *culturally sustaining* practices, and (4) the successful redesign of practices and programs requires practitioners to work in solidarity with allies and educators across race and culture. Based on these four principles, I include in this book theoretical frameworks, narratives, SEL activities, and opportunities for you to connect with others who are reading this work as a first step to redesigning educational practices. From my years of training educators on racially and culturally meaningful work, the four aforementioned principles were central to work redesign. This book is a first step in the process of redesigning current practices. I wish you well as you engage with the SEL activities within this book, reflect on racial and cultural memories, and prepare for antiracist and culturally sustaining programming.

Chapter 1: Antiracist Education

During the afternoon of April 22, 1993, Stephen Lawrence, an 18-year-old Black British teenager, waited at a London bus stop with his friend Duwayne Brooks. While waiting for the bus, Stephen walked into the street to glance down the road to see if a bus was coming, since they were in a hurry to get home. While Stephen searched for the bus, Duwayne called out to Stephen, asking if any buses were approaching. In response to Duwayne's call, a White teenager who was with a group of White youth shouted, "What? What, nigger?" The group of White teenagers quickly crossed the street, and one of them stabbed Stephen twice, once on each side of the front of his body. During the stabbing, Duwayne sprinted away, yelling for Stephen to follow him. As Stephen fell from the stabbing and as Duwayne sprinted away, the bus they awaited approached the stop, and the witnesses of the murder boarded. Stephen eventually found a way to get to his feet and ran over 100 yards in the direction of his friend Duwayne, before collapsing to his death. His point of collapse is now marked with a granite memorial stone placed into the pavement (*Inquiry, Stephen Lawrence*, 1999, Sections 1.1-1.12).

Initially, no one was convicted for Stephen's murder, which was "simply and solely and unequivocally motivated by racism" (*Inquiry, Stephen Lawrence*, 1999, Section 1.11). Four years later, in response to demands by Stephen's parents for justice and a public hearing, an incoming government in 1997 met the Lawrences' request. The *Stephen Lawrence Inquiry Report* was the result of the hearing. Gillborn (2006) contends that "*The Stephen Lawrence Inquiry Report*, and the consequent public debates, provided the closest British parallel yet to the kinds of national furor over racism that were sparked in the US by the Rodney King affair and the O.J. Simpson trials" (p. 14). The inquiry stated loudly and boldly that institutional racism was prevalent in government agencies, including law enforcement, education, and health services (Gillborn, 2006). Regarding the case of Stephen Lawrence, Sivanandan (2000) commented, "The unrelenting struggle of the Lawrences' has put institutional racism back on the agenda . . . . They changed the whole discourse on race relations and made the government and the media and the people of this country acknowledge that there is a deep, ingrained, systematic racism in the institutions and structures of this society" (p. 7). The Lawrence case and the evidence that it generated concerning structural racism provided longer and stronger legs for antiracist practices and policies in Britain.

To be sure, antiracist education emerged in the twentieth century in the United Kingdom in response to deliberate racism (Carr & Lund, 2009); it became popular in the United States during the civil rights movement, and while the concept appeared to lose traction in various fields in education over time (Williams, 1999), it has recently experienced an explosion in curiosity and interest among educators. For example, educators have flooded social media with images, quotes, and commentary from the best-selling book, *How to Become an Antiracist*, by Ibram X. Kendi (2019). Even more, practitioners acknowledge the importance of becoming antiracist practitioners, evidenced by the increased number of webinars and Zoom meetings addressing the integration of antiracist principles in schools.

You might wonder exactly how antiracist education is defined. According to Banks and Banks (1993), leading scholars in multicultural education, antiracist education refers to practices that seek to "eliminate institutionalized racism from the school and society and to help individuals develop antiracist attitudes" (p. 357). Carr and Lund (2009) contend that antiracist education "emphasizes the need to address systemic barriers that cultivate and sustain racism, particularly within educational settings" (p. 48). They maintain that, at the theoretical and practical levels, antiracist education aligns with social justice and equity work. Essentially, antiracist education explicitly disrupts oppressive and racist structures on both an individual and systemic level, by examining how racist beliefs and attitudes empower institutional racism by "supporting and maintaining disadvantage and advantage along racial lines" (Escayg, 2018, p. 16).

It is necessary to understand how antiracist scholars define racists and antiracists within the context of antiracist work. Kendi (2019) argues that a racist is "one who is supporting a racist policy through their actions or inaction or expressing a racist idea" (p. 13). Contrarily, he defines an antiracist as "one who is supporting an antiracist policy through their actions or expressing an antiracist idea" (p. 20). According to Kendi, racist policies are synonymous with other terms such as *institutional racism, structural racism,* and *systemic racism,* and that the term *racist policy* explicitly addresses racist policies that create racial inequity; in other words, the phrase speaks directly to the problem. Kendi (2019) maintains that "racism is a powerful collection of racist policies that lead to racial inequity and are substantiated by racist ideas" (p. 20). He maintains that, in order to create equitable opportunities, we must identify our position as racists or antiracists; he contends that there is no middle ground—a perspective that some educators have rejected. In his words,

What's the problem with being not racist? It is a claim that signifies neutrality: I am not a racist, but neither am I aggressively against racism.

To this point, Kendi (2019) argues

The opposite of *racist* isn't '*not racist.*' It is antiracist (p. 9).

He maintains that one either believes inequality is a result of groups of people—a racist ideology—or that inequality is the result of power and racist policies—an antiracist ideology. Essentially, he recommends that individuals develop an antiracist mindset and engage in antiracist practices in order to resist injustice.

What Are You Teaching for and What Are You Teaching Against?

Educator and activist William Ayers argues that, while teaching, we must ask ourselves, "What am I teaching for? What am I teaching against?" (Ayers, 2004, p. 11). Considering the racial tension that we are experiencing in our country, I ask you to wrestle with those questions. What are you teaching for? What are you teaching against? As for me, I am teaching against racist ideas, policies, practices, and programs, while preparing agentic students to resist, reject, and challenge racist programming that racist scholars designed to oppress them. In addition to asking ourselves, "What am I teaching for and against?" I suggest that we ask ourselves a more controversial question: "What side of the racist and antiracist coin do I stand on?" When answering this question, it is important to note that, as Kendi (2019) suggests, there is no middle ground; we are either aggressively disrupting racism or we are turning a blind eye to it. If your response is that you side with antiracist principles and you identify as an antiracist educator, then my questions to you are, "What are you doing that makes you an antiracist educator?" and "In what ways are you contributing to antiracist programming?"

Antiracist Education and Culturally Sustaining Practices

As a researcher-practitioner, I have found that many educators perceive race and culture synonymously. From these experiences, I argue that school leaders who desire to design antiracist educational practices and culturally sustaining programming must offer professional development for practitioners that addresses antiracism and culturally sustaining teaching, while at the same time provide the context of justice and equity. Here is why: If practitioners receive training on antiracism and racial equity work, they will have knowledge of racial-justice principles but will lack knowledge on how to implement activities that may sustain the cultural values, assets, languages, literacies, and identities of students of color, which is an equity and justice issue.

On the other hand, if practitioners receive in-service training on the topic of culture and culturally sustaining practices without acknowledging race and racism, it is possible that practitioners will continue to view race and culture synonymously, which can result in well-intentioned, yet stereotypical and prejudicial actions when designing programming. For example, it is possible for practitioners who perceive race and culture synonymously to learn about hip-hop pedagogy, and then make the leap to, "Oh! All Black boys love hip-hop!" They may clumsily design a racially stereotypical lesson around that – an idea that started in a good place, but was then executed poorly. I have provided culturally sustaining groups and activities for thousands of students during my tenure as a school psychologist, and while a great majority of Black students embraced hip-hop, there were many who despised it. Therefore, creating inclusive programming and policies requires an antiracial, cultural, *and* equitable understanding of teaching and learning. From this perspective, then, an antiracist and culturally sustaining educator is one who actively disrupts racist policies, agendas, and practices; an antiracist and culturally sustaining educator actively seeks ways not only to create culturally *relevant* and *responsive* activities in the classroom, but also seeks to *sustain*, foster, and perpetuate the cultures, languages, literacies, and identities of students of color. This means that antiracist educators resist employing the cultural assets of students of color for the sole purpose of "engaging" them during instructional time or creating culturally responsive activities to manage them during school hours. Furthermore, antiracist and culturally sustaining educators do not "use" the cultures, literacies, and languages of students for the sole purpose of strengthening teacher-student relationships.

When antiracist educators implement culturally relevant and responsive practices, they do so because they desire to strengthen the ethnic, racial, and cultural identities of students, not weaken them; they desire to inspire students to embrace their dialects and languages, including African American Vernacular English, not reject them. Through their actions, antiracist and culturally sustaining educators develop antiracist students by emphasizing principles of equity, inclusion, and justice in both theory and practice. While some educators are tooting the "antiracist" horn, I argue that the telltale sign of true antiracism is disruption: disrupting the status quo, disrupting practices that exclude the cultural assets and values of Black and Brown students, and disrupting norms and policies that racist scholars designed to oppress students of color—policies and practices that measure their cognitive abilities and behaviors based on Eurocentric standards, values, norms, and frameworks.

What's in the Name "Antiracist Education?"

In his article *Branding Culturally Relevant Teaching: A Call for Remixes*, Sharroky Hollie (2019) shares an experience of reviewing an article titled *Culturally Relevant Leadership: What Does it Take?* (p. 32). While reading the article, Hollie noticed that although the title of the article included the words *culturally relevant*, the author did not address assumptions, principles, and practices associated with culturally relevant pedagogy. Rather, the author sprinkled buzzwords such as "equity," "culturally sensitivity," and "inclusivity" (p. 32) throughout the paper without explicitly stating ways to promote and apply culturally relevant principles for leadership. From this experience, Hollie asked, "What's in a name?" (p. 32). He problematized and interrogated the tendency to throw around popular terms, phrases, and names—which is akin to spewing phrases such as antiracist education, culturally relevant pedagogy, culturally responsive teaching, and culturally sustaining practices—without explicitly acknowledging and adhering to the application of the terms. To this point, I challenge my brothers and sisters to resist calling themselves antiracist educators if they are not actively *applying* antiracist principles of justice, inclusion, and equity. I challenge my brothers and sisters to resist spewing antiracist phrases and terminology without action.

I wrote *Redesign* to support teachers in their efforts to redesign practices and policies in order to reject racist programming and to prepare for culturally sustaining practices. *Redesign* is a first step, a practical approach, to designing antiracist practices and policies. As a school psychologist and interventionist, I have been a part of many professional development sessions that address race, racism, and culture, and as a researcher-practitioner who trains teachers on culturally responsive and sustaining teaching, I have immersed myself in culturally meaningful scholarship. I'll admit that I agree with some books, articles, and trainers, while I cringe at others. What is clear to me, however, is that designing culturally sustaining, inclusive, and antiracist practices begins with self-reflection.

Although designing culturally sustaining, inclusive, and equitable practices starts with reflection, preparing students of color to process racially traumatic experiences and to resist oppression requires practitioners to *apply* theory: it requires action. Therefore, I argue that it is time for practitioners to move past rhetoric and philosophy. The time calls for educators to roll up their sleeves, to challenge racist ideologies, policies, and practices, and to implement activities in the classroom in ways that prepare students of color to engage in agentic actions of liberation. *Redesign: An SEL Toolkit to Designing Culturally Sustaining and Antiracist Practices* prepares administrators and practitioners for this call.

Chapter 2: Reflection

Beliefs and attitudes precede instruction (Abacioglu, Volman, & Fischer, 2019; Gay, 2018; Rychly & Graves, 2012). From this perspective, our lived experiences influence our beliefs and attitudes; in turn, our beliefs and attitudes influence educational practices. Therefore, our beliefs around race, culture, and equity influence the kinds of services we provide for students of color. Practitioners who believe that designing inclusive programming is essential to the wellbeing of students are more prone to implementing equitable practices for all students than practitioners who do not share the same views and values. Practitioners who believe that antiracist education—education that disrupts racist practices and policies (Kendi, 2019)—is essential to preparing productive citizens will be more prone to challenging, critiquing, and resisting racist policies, practices, and norms than are practitioners who do not share the same views and values. Thus, this book sets practitioners on the path of redesign by starting with a reflection on lived racial and cultural experiences from a personal, historical approach. A personal historical approach refers to our own personal history, our lived experiences.

For years, practitioners, administrators, and students have asked what inspires me to design activities that sustain the cultures, literacies, and languages of students. Although they all used different phrases, terms, and ways of inquiring about my journey with race, culture, and education, they all expressed interest in my racial and cultural history. They wanted me to retrace for them experiences that inspire my current beliefs, attitudes, and perspectives concerning culturally sustaining, inclusive, and equitable practices. After learning about my work, you may have the same questions as my students and colleagues about my history. There is no better way of understanding our current perspectives on race and culture than examining our own histories with race and culture. Therefore, I will model the importance of starting with history when redesigning work-related activities. I will do this by retracing my journey with race and culture in order to reveal how I became an antiracist school psychologist and interventionist determined to disrupt racist policies and practices. I will begin with my history and recall the most significant event that set me on a course of educational redesign.

My Journey

In 2006, while a graduate student at Marshall University, I met Dr. Arthur, who changed my life. Dr. Arthur was an African professor. He was a brilliant scholar. He was my mentor. One morning, while I was sitting in the education conference room waiting for my class to start and sipping a freshly brewed cup of coffee, Dr. Arthur entered the room, dragging the familiar worn, black-and-gray rolling cart he used to transport stacks of articles, books, and a radio across campus. He hurried through the door, aggressively jerking his cart so it would not jam in the entrance as he closed the door behind him.

"Good morning, Dwayne," he said. "I am so happy that you are here. I've been meaning to ask you a few questions. If you have a minute, come to my office—won't take long at all."

I finished what was left of my coffee, quickly stuffed the articles I planned to read in my bag, and walked in his direction, all while thinking about the assignments I was supposed to complete while waiting in the conference room. I entered his office, where annotated papers and articles covered his desk and floor. Before I had a chance to sit down, Dr. Arthur began asking an array of questions about the program in which I was enrolled.

"Dwayne, how is your school psychology program coming?"

"Aw, things are coming along well, Dr. Arthur. I am reading a lot, learning a ton of theories, and reading about psychologists who contributed to their field."

He then began to quiz me, which was strange; it was something he had not done before. "Dwayne, name five European psychologists who have contributed to their field."

I was excited to provide a response, for my aim was to impress Dr. Arthur, my mentor, with the knowledge I was learning in the program. I responded confidently: "Psychologists who contributed to the field, okay, cool . . . You got . . . you got . . . You got Sigmund Freud, Ivan Pavlov, B. F. Skinner, John B. Watson, William James . . . that's five! But I can name more. Albert Bandura, Alfred Adler, Abraham Maslow, Carl Rogers, Carl Jung, Erik Erikson, Jean Piaget, Wilhelm Wundt, Kurt Lewin. . ."

After I named more than fifteen psychologists, he interrupted me.

"Very good, Dwayne. Now name one, one African American psychologist who contributed to their field."

My excitement ceased as he stared convincingly into my eyes.

"African American psychologist? We, we—"I stammered. "We don't talk about African American psychologists."

"Dwayne, name one culturally responsive theory that you might consider when working with African American students."

"Culturally responsive theory? I am not familiar with any culturally responsive theories to consider when working with African American students. We don't talk about culturally responsive theories . . ."

Dr. Arthur could obviously tell it was the first time I'd heard the phrase "culturally responsive," as I stumbled over my words and repeated the phrase.

He then snatched my attention. "Dwayne, it is clear that you are very knowledgeable about Eurocentric theories and European psychologists. You just named over fifteen European psychologists, but you cannot even name one African American psychologist."

He became progressively passionate and gradually spoke as if my life depended on every word that he uttered, "Dwayne, you must do more. You must read books written by Black psychologists. You must read scholarship, Dwayne, written by scholars of color. You must read about how to boost engagement among culturally diverse learners and allow their experiences to guide instruction." Then Dr. Arthur said something that changed my life. "Dwayne, if you graduate from this university only with knowledge of Eurocentric values, Eurocentric theories, Eurocentric thinking—you will graduate as a Black psychologist, with a Eurocentric mindset. And you will perceive Black and Brown students similar to how your textbooks described them."

He eventually concluded his message, "Dwayne, if you remember anything that I have shared with you this morning, remember this: In order to engage students of color at their highest potential, you must begin with their culture. You must create opportunities for students to learn through their own lenses and through their own experiences. You must consider their values and interests when working with students in school. Begin with their culture."

I often reflect on my experiences with Dr. Arthur. If it were not for that meeting, it is possible I would not have accomplished what I have in the field. Dr. Arthur made me think about a depressing reality, one that illustrates the importance of culturally sustaining, inclusive, and equitable work. Although I have a bachelor's and master's degree in psychology, along with an educational specialist degree, I do not recall ever addressing the accomplishments and contributions of psychologists and educators of color during these years. Whenever we talked about students of color, we talked about how they score standard deviations below White students on standardized tests.

I recall learning that many students of color do not perform well on the verbal sections of intelligence tests for various reasons. When I started practicing as a school psychologist, I often became ecstatic when students of color performed well on standardized tests. I was ecstatic because it was contrary to what I read in books and articles during my programs. Shamefully, during my early years as a school psychologist, I evaluated students of color from a deficit, racist mindset.

I remember the experience of evaluating a Black high school male student as if it happened yesterday. When I walked to his classroom to get him, I was sure that he, a Black kid from an impoverished community, was going to perform below standards and qualify for special education services. As I got to the verbal section of the IQ test, I was stunned as he correctly answered items that I asked of him. I couldn't wait to score his protocol; I was eager to learn how he performed. I walked the young man back to class after the evaluation and ran, literally, back to my office to score his protocol, his results. To my surprise, the young man scored in the high average range, with impressive sub-scores across subareas. My attitudes, beliefs, and perspectives about my own people were racist, if we define racism as "a belief that race is the primary determinant of human traits and capacities and that racial differences produce an inherent superiority of a particular race" (Racism, 2020; Merriam Webster). It was evident that, although I cared greatly and deeply about people of color, my people, I retained racist beliefs, attitudes, and perspectives about the abilities of children and youth of color. I learned this way of thinking from books and articles I read during the many years of undergraduate and graduate school. I held these beliefs even though my master's level thesis was on culture and student engagement. The reality is that my entire training from undergraduate through graduate school was steeped in Eurocentric theories, and much of the scholarship that I read about students of color was rooted in racist, deficit thinking.

Before I could work effectively with students of color, before I could appreciate my own people's abilities, their literacies, their languages, their ways of being, I had to engage in deep reflection and reject the racist theories and explanations that I had read over the years that subliminally shaped my thinking about students of color. My reflection led to a redesign in the ways in which I evaluated and provided educational programming for students of color. Note that, even as a person of color, I engaged in racist practices. I practiced as a racist educator, although I am certainly not racist against my own people. Is that even possible? Is that a thing? Carter G Woodson explained this phenomenon in his book *The Miseducation of the Negro*. Woodson (2006) commented that African Americans enter predominantly White institutions as Black men and Black women, but leave as well-trained White people. His observation describes training steeped in Eurocentric values, assumptions, and beliefs which all students—and students of color, in particular—receive in graduate level programs.

Antiracist Education, Practices, and Policies

Redesigning educational work begins with rejecting the racist belief that Eurocentric values and theoretical assumptions apply to all students, no matter their race, culture, and worldviews. As educators, we often practice based on how training programs, mentors, and advisors taught us; we practice consistent with scholarship that we read during our education. In addition, we practice based on our historical experiences with race and culture that influence our beliefs, attitudes, and perspectives concerning race, culture, and people of color. Similar to my experiences with evaluating students of color, many educators currently engage in racist practices unknowingly, while some, perhaps, do so knowingly. I wrote *Redesign* to provide opportunities for practitioners to think critically about their experiences, to engage in practical, reflective activities as a first step to redesigning educational practices, and to challenge, criticize, and reject racist policies and programs that may find their way in classrooms. I argue that in order for us to revamp our practices in ways that are culturally sustaining, inclusive, and equitable, it is critical that we identify a theoretical framework that will guide us along the way. Thus, the successful redesign of practice requires reflection, theory, and action. Excluding any one of these components may perpetuate racist, oppressive practices. Excluding any one of these components is a recipe for disaster.

Chapter 3: The Framework

"There is nothing more practical than good theory."
~Kurt Lewin

As a practitioner, I get it. I get that many of my brothers and sisters in the field despise theory. Many of us are tired of it. We are tired of reading books that are beautifully written but terribly ineffective at helping us design and redesign school-based practices in ways that are culturally sustaining, inclusive and equitable. We are tired of spending endless hours sitting in professional development workshops, where speakers make promises such as "by the end of this session, you will recognize how to design effective practices for culturally diverse learners," only to leave the training with more concepts and theoretical principles to think through. We are tired of being told, after an in-service, "You are the work, so do something when you return to your classroom."

We need direction. We need practices. We need support. We work with students who require the best interventions right now—not tomorrow, not next week, not next month, not next year. Right now. As a practitioner, I agree that we must act swiftly and carefully, or we may miss opportunities to engage with our students. Many of our students are transient, and so it can be a now-you-see-them-now-you-don't experience. I understand that the time to act is now.

As a researcher-practitioner, however, I also understand the importance of theory and theoretical frameworks. Theory guides us through the process of designing effective practices. To be sure, theory is just as important as practice. I'll share an example to illustrate the importance of theory and practice.

I recently purchased a black rising desk for my home office. It is nice and has many features. Prior to assembling the desk, I went online to read the assembly reviews. I wanted to see if others had problems with the assembly and to see if there were any steps that I might run into that might give me a challenge. I was hoping to get some tips before cracking the box open. And just as I suspected, there were many reviews that complained about various steps in the assembly process. One review stated, "Assembly is easy, but when you come to step four of the process, it is very challenging. The directions do not provide the best instructions on how to assemble the desktop table to the rising frame. I give the desk a five-star rating, but I give the instructions a 3.5."

Okay, great.

I began to assemble the desk, and just as the review stated, step four was challenging. I read and reread the directions, but they were ineffective at guiding me through this step. It took me fifteen more minutes to figure this step out. However, I was able to assemble the desk successfully because I was able to think ahead, reread the instructions, process what the desk was designed to do, reference the picture on the box, and use context clues from other steps to direct me along the way, and—voila!—I figured it out. I assembled the desk and it worked perfectly.

Now get this. Considering I assembled the desk and understood the assembly process and various parts of the design, if a component of the desk stops working, I will know how to remove and replace the piece that doesn't work. This would not be the case if I had purchased the desk pre-assembled. Okay, my point? I was able to assemble the desk because I had a conceptual and visual model that guided me through the process. Although one step gave me a challenge, other steps and images helped me along the way. Theory works the same way. It guides us. It directs us. It informs us.

And guess what. When we apply theory in the classroom, we may certainly experience the same struggle I experienced when assembling my rising desk. That is, the theoretical principles that we attempt to apply may not help us design the exact kind of support that we envision the first time we apply them. But if we have knowledge of the assumptions of the theory and have key concepts and some direction in mind, we will be able to apply what we know about the theory, instead of practicing without any direction. Even more, if we apply theory in the process of redesigning practices, and the intervention is ineffective, then we can go back to the drawing board and resketch our design, hopefully with the assistance of students, in order to redesign our practice based on our goals. Eventually, by focusing on key principles and trusting the process, we will experience a voila! moment. My point is, as practitioners, we need theory to guide our activities. Theory may not provide step-by-step assembly directions for our practices, but it will certainly guide us in the process of redesign. Considering the importance of theory, this book draws from cultural historical activity theory (CHAT) and culturally sustaining pedagogy (CSP), theories that I will briefly describe next.

Cultural Historical Activity Theory

Cultural historical activity theory (CHAT) is an analytical tool that practitioners can use to examine current practices. CHAT is a tool that helps practitioners examine classroom rules, resources used in a lesson, and purpose of a lesson. Using CHAT, practitioners examine the kinds of cultural tools they use to engage students when delivering instruction; based on the data they generate from CHAT, practitioners can then determine if their instructional tools clash with the cultural values and interests of students of color. Essentially, CHAT is a tool that helps practitioners analyze how people and organizations learn new things and evolve over time as a result of resolving tensions and challenges that arise in schools in general and classrooms in particular. To be sure, CHAT was not designed specifically for school practitioners, but practitioners can benefit from using the framework to examine their practices in order to determine if their current instructional designs acknowledge and integrate the cultural values, assets, and lived experiences of students of color.

CHAT originated with the seminal work of Lev Vygotsky and his students. Although decades of research support the framework, I will share only the assumptions of the theory. Assumptions and key principles help us understand the big ideas of a theory. Each term in the phrase *cultural historical activity theory* has a specific meaning that represents key aspects of the theory (Gretschel, Ramugondo, & Galvaan, 2015, p. 52), and understanding key principles help us think about instruction and our practices from a cultural and historical lens. Next, I will share exactly what each term means in "cultural historical activity theory," as each term has implications for practice.

Cultural

Cultural refers to the notion that culture shapes us; cultural experiences influence our worldviews and perspectives in life. From this view, we engage through culture, we form relationships through culture, and we design rules and norms by using cultural references and cultural tools. Culture shapes all instructional practices, rules, policies, and norms. In American schools, Eurocentric values influence rules, policies, and practices. Consequently, when culturally diverse learners show up and engage in classrooms that are shaped by Eurocentric values and norms, their behaviors and ways of being often fall outside Eurocentric cultural boundaries; as a result, practitioners tend to deem the actions of culturally diverse learners to be disruptive, deviant, and disrespectful. Accordingly, cultural tension arises as a result of clashes between the dominant, Eurocentric cultural values of the classroom and the diverse body of cultural values that students embrace and demonstrate in those spaces. In the same way, students of color may disengage or become disruptive because of cultural clashes they experience with racially and culturally insensitive curricula. In many cases, students are kicked out of the classroom, given detentions and suspensions, and referred for special education services in response to cultural clashes. Therefore, when staff refers a student for specialized services, it is critical that team members tease out whether the perceived deficit in question stems from a disability or if the concern represents a cultural clash between the student's culture and the dominant culture of the school and classroom.

I should also mention the tools that social workers and school psychologists use to evaluate students are also rooted in Eurocentric values, and so practitioners must consider the ways in which their evaluations are culturally biased. Therefore, school leaders must provide training to examine the role culture plays in the disproportionate number of Black and Brown students who are suspended, the number of Black and Brown students who are referred for special education services, and the number of Black and Brown students who qualify for special education services. A review of data from almost any school district in America with students of color will reveal the racist practices in disciplining and evaluating Black and Brown students for special education services, policies and practices that require a redesign.

Historical

Historical in CHAT refers to the notion that people are connected to and influenced by their histories and that their history influences how they perceive the world. Contrary to this view, school-based practitioners are often taught to focus on the "here and now." CHAT implies that students may act a certain way in the present moment in response to their personal histories (including histories with traumatic events and experiences) just as they may act in certain ways based on cultural histories (life experiences that pertain to the treatment of their racial and cultural group members). For example, when White teachers read books that contain the word "nigger," or play audio books that speak the word, Black kids may respond a certain way in that moment (here and now), based on historical knowledge of what happened to their racial group members in the past. This principle does not imply, however, that cultural histories "make" Black kids act in certain ways. It does imply, however, that students may be sensitive to historical events that are associated with their cultural and racial group members.

Activity

Activity refers to the collective interaction of people shaped and reshaped by history and culture. Within any organization, team members engage in specific actions in order to accomplish short-and long-term goals. Activity, then, according to CHAT, refers to all actions and interactions that team members engage in to accomplish a task (Engestrom, 2000); stated differently, the interaction among group members to accomplish a task refers to an activity. School stakeholders, including students, parents, practitioners, administrators, and community members, interact within activity systems to provide the highest level of instruction for students. In activity systems, activity members construct rules, use cultural tools to teach and process relevant content, and devise goals for the system, although goals may shift, based on the needs of activity members and the system.

School-based activity systems include general and special education classrooms, counseling groups—including social emotional learning and trauma-informed groups—restorative circles, multitiered systems of support, problem-solving teams, special education evaluation and eligibility teams, and so on. CHAT principles contend that all activity systems (all of the classrooms, groups, and teams where people interact in schools) are rooted in culture, considering activity systems are composed of cultural group members who interact, share perspectives, and design, based on cultural worldviews.

The problem in activity systems in most schools is that although activity systems are composed of racially and culturally diverse members, instructional strategies, tools, rules, perspectives, and ways of being are often rooted in Eurocentric values, principles, and ways of thinking. Redesign in activity systems, then, requires what CHAT refers to as multivoice systems, where the voices of all members act in agentic ways to solve the problems of the system, where all members construct knowledge based on their cultural ways of processing, and where all members interpret, view, and suggest solutions based on their worldviews.

A multivoice system would also encourage activity members to show up as themselves rather than as someone else. I will use an example to illustrate this point. In my years of experience working in schools—eleven years at the time of this publication—I have noticed that some of my Black colleagues interacted with me one way when it was just the colleague and me, but interacted with me differently when we were in the presence of White people.

I jokingly identify these kinds of colleagues as "Black-White" people. They change their voices in meetings when sharing their perspective, over-articulate the sounds of letters when they speak, with the hope that their White bosses and colleagues will perceive them in a particular way, and do other things to fit into Eurocentric systems. Of course, this is my own observation and interpretation as a Black man who embraces and speaks African American Vernacular English; it is my observation and interpretation based on my own cultural perspectives and ways of viewing that kind of behavior and social interaction. Nonetheless, a multivoice system would encourage my Black colleagues to show up as themselves. Throughout my years as a practitioner, when I attended meetings with my White and Black-White colleagues, I was sure to present as myself. My point is Eurocentrism dominates activity systems in American institutions, including schools. Activity systems in schools demand a redesign in order to create culturally sustaining, inclusive, and equitable practices. In the same way, my Black brothers and sisters—and all my other racially different allies who show up as someone they are not—require redesigns in their mindsets and ways of viewing the world in order to design equitable programming. They require a redesign in their ways of thinking in order to model for students the importance of embracing their own heritages, languages, literacies, cultures, and ways of being.

Theory

Theory refers to philosophical principles that guide practices. CHAT is a practitioner-based theory that leads to designing and redesigning work-related activities and offers tools to analyze challenges within work-related practices; it provides tools to resolve those challenges in order to redesign activities based on the needs of a system. Key terms that comprise CHAT include activity, activity systems, multivoice systems, and history. This book draws from CHAT in that we will

- engage in activities (in the "Activities" section, chapter four of this book),
- use tools to reflect on our racial and cultural lived experiences,
- construct a racial and cultural journey map of our lived experiences with race and culture,
- use SEL competencies as tools to guide our reflection, and
- employ the principle of history as we review our lived experiences from a historical timeline.

In terms of activity system, I encourage all readers to join my *Redesign* Facebook group. Our group will function as an activity system, where all members show up as themselves, use their cultural literacies, languages, and ways of being to redesign their own classroom practices, and design antiracist activities. Along with SEL and CHAT theoretical principles, this book draws from culturally sustaining pedagogy, which I will briefly discuss now.

Culturally Sustaining Pedagogy

Culturally *relevant* teaching and culturally *responsive* teaching are familiar phrases within K-12 education. I'm sure most practitioners have heard of one or the other. However, less familiar is culturally *sustaining* pedagogy. I'll describe culturally sustaining pedagogy as the cousin of culturally relevant and culturally responsive teaching. Gloria Ladson-Billings calls culturally sustaining pedagogy a needed remix of her original culturally relevant theory (Ladson-Billings, 2014), endorsing it as a legitimate theory and pedagogy.

While both culturally relevant and culturally responsive teaching have become popular phrases in K-12 education, and while the practices are supported by decades of research, scholars question if the theories and practices are sufficient at fostering and sustaining the literacies and languages of youth of color (Paris & Alim, 2017). To this end, Paris (2012) argues for *culturally sustaining pedagogies* as an alternative practice to culturally relevant and culturally responsive pedagogies (p. 95). In his words: "The term culturally sustaining requires that our pedagogies be more than responsive and relevant to the cultural experiences and practices of young people—it requires that they [our practices] support young people in sustaining the cultural and linguistic competence of their communities while simultaneously offering access to dominant cultural competence" (p. 95). From this view, culturally sustaining pedagogy seeks to perpetuate, foster, and sustain the languages, literacies, identities, and cultural ways of being of youth of color.

While culturally *responsive* teaching principles guide much of my work as a school psychologist and interventionist, this book draws from culturally *sustaining* principles, considering it is the most current remix within the cultural relevance tradition, and considering it is consistent with my research on redesigning systems. To this end, I agree with Paris and Alim (2017) and Ladson-Billings (2014) in that the time calls for practitioners to engage in practices that are relevant and responsive, but also seek to foster and sustain the literacies, languages, and identities that youth of color bring to the classroom. In other words, it is time for educators to create activities that foster and sustain the literacies and languages that students of color bring to school from communities that are rich in expressive language, rich in kinesthetic movement, and rich in wordplay, among other assets. Thus, when you read the phrase culturally sustaining practices throughout this book, the phrase refers to designing activities that are not only relevant and responsive to the lives of students, but also seek to foster racial and cultural identities, literacies, and languages of students as a goal of instructional programming.

Social Emotional Learning and the Toolkit

Finally, and as I alluded earlier, in addition to principles associated with CHAT and CSP, this book draws from CASEL's (2020) five SEL competencies as a guiding framework for reflective activities. These competencies include *self-awareness, self-management, social awareness, relationship skills,* and *responsible decision-making.* Using CASEL's (2020) framework, I will guide you through the process of reflecting on race and culture from a personal, historical perspective in order to reflect on racial and cultural experiences, and how these experiences might influence your current ideas and attitudes about education, practice, race, culture, and students of color. I then guide you through the process of examining tensions and challenges that interfere with redesigning inequitable practices. These processes are associated with the CHAT principles that I shared earlier, and I pair them with social emotional competencies that will guide us through the process of designing equitable practices.

Culturally meaningful SEL activities in this book will prepare you to think critically about redesigning your current practices in ways that consider the lived experiences of your students. The most essential component of this process is reflecting on experiences, beliefs, attitudes, and practices from a historical perspective in order to identify *contradictions* or challenges to designing culturally sustaining, inclusive, and equitable practices. In order to gain from this book, it is critically important that you understand the notion of contradictions as they are described here. Briefly stated, contradictions are tensions and challenges that prevent us from designing and redesigning our work. In the field of education, they may be personal or systemic challenges that interfere with our ability to construct antiracist programming.

The following are common contradictions that I have observed when training practitioners on redesigning their work: practitioners articulate the need and desire to redesign their practices, but continue to implement instructional practices that are rooted in Eurocentric culture, values, and thinking. Another contradiction that I found when working with practitioners is that some identify themselves as culturally responsive educators, but do not place the cultural assets and lived experiences of students at the center of instruction. These are critical contradictions that prevent the formation of culturally responsive programming. The most recent contradiction that I have observed from browsing social media is that educators, inspired by antiracist work, identify themselves as antiracist educators, yet they employ problem-solving practices that originated from the minds of racist scholars who believed that students of color and students from impoverished backgrounds were innately inferior and inherently incapable of succeeding at high levels in the classroom. We cannot be antiracist educators and continue to employ practices and problem-solving models that employ racist principles that stem from deficit-based thinking. This is a discrepancy and contradiction that will harm students of color.

If we are to become antiracist educators, we will need to redesign the ways in which we implement practices. We will also have to revisit school policies from a historical perspective and examine how our practices and policies are biased and racist toward students of color. Contradictions—for example, identifying oneself as an antiracist educator yet employing racist problem-solving tactics—are perhaps the number one reason practitioners are unable to design culturally sustaining, inclusive, and equitable practices. This is why in the activities section of this book, I focus specifically on reflection as a first step in the process of work redesign, using SEL competencies and practical activities in order to examine your lived experiences with race and culture. I then guide you through the process of examining your current practices in order to identify contradictions in becoming an antiracist educator.

Redesign Facebook Online Community of Practice

It was author Ruqaiyyah Waris Maqsood who said, "It is wonderful to be in solidarity with another big group of people." Redesigning current practices require educators to be in solidarity with groups of people. While this book guides you through the process of interrogating your beliefs and attitudes from a racial, cultural, and equity lens, the next step in the process requires you to redesign your work using theoretical principles I have shared in this book. To guide you along the way, I have organized an online community of practice Facebook page for readers to connect with other educators who are reading this book and designing culturally sustaining and antiracist practices. The Facebook community of practice page is called *Redesign An SEL Toolkit*.

You might wonder what communities of practice are. Communities of practice are "groups of people who share a concern or a passion for something they do and learn how to do it better as they interact regularly" (Etienne Wenger, 2009, p. 1). In the *Redesign* community of practice Facebook page, we—parents, community leaders, practitioners, and administrators—are a community who shares resources, lived experiences, and instructional strategies to better design culturally sustaining, inclusive, and equitable practices for culturally diverse learners across grade levels. Additionally, in our community of practice Facebook group, I provide additional coaching on how to design or redesign classroom practices in order to prepare you for antiracist programming. Coaching will involve direct support on what you should do next after completing the activities in this book, how to start discussions around race, culture, inclusion, and equity within your classrooms with students, and how to bring culturally sustaining, inclusive, and equitable approaches to your problem-solving teams.

Coaching addresses application, practical strategies that you can use to build yourself as a culturally competent, antiracist educator as well as strategies you can employ to engage students in the classroom. As a special bonus, I have colleagues who are teachers, administrators, psychologists, and social workers who are designing culturally sustaining and antiracist practices who will share their work. All are currently practicing at the ground level with us, in schools around the country. I am currently training them on my redesign scholarship, and they will join me in sharing experiences and providing feedback in the *Redesign* Facebook group. Designing culturally sustaining, inclusive, and equitable practices is a journey, and I guarantee if you complete the activities in the following section and follow up with direct coaching from me and other educators in the field doing antiracist work, you will design and implement some of the most engaging practices you have ever implemented. Even better, you will design practices that place issues of race, culture, and equity at the center of instruction that will prepare students to resist oppressive practices.

Chapter 4: SEL Activities and Racial History

As I articulated earlier in this book, redesigning educational practices and policies is a process that begins with self-reflection. I agree with Gay (2018) that practitioners must interrogate their beliefs and attitudes when redesigning instructional practices, considering beliefs and attitudes influence actions. In this section, I employ CASEL's (2020) SEL framework as a guiding tool to reflect on racial and cultural experiences. I adapt SEL definitions in culturally meaningful ways; I use the culturally adapted definitions to guide the activities. In addition to CASEL's (2020) SEL framework, I employ cultural historical activity theory's (CHAT) principles of historicity and tools to help us pull from our subconscious significant historical events from our development (see chapter three for a discussion on CHAT).

The philosophical principle of historicity (Engestrom, 2001, p. 136) contends that, in order to understand a current problem, we must start from its history. In order to understand our beliefs and attitudes concerning race and culture—and how we provide instruction in the classroom when working with students of color—we must begin with our personal history and retrace our racial and cultural experiences. Additionally, the principle of historicity maintains that we must examine the training we received in teacher training programs and examine the theories that we learned about children of color, their parents, cultures, languages, and communities in order to best understand our perceptions of them; examining our training and pairing it with our personal history with race and culture helps us understand how we have become the educators we are today. According to CHAT, we use cultural tools to work on our environment to accomplish tasks. I use the concept of cultural tools as I guide you through the process of creating a racial-cultural journey map (see Activity 1.1). We then use the map as a culturally meaningful tool to complete subsequent activities. Finally, I draw from Paris's (2012) culturally sustaining pedagogy to examine the ways in which we sustain the cultures, languages, literacies, and identities of students of color.

I include multiple activities within the *self-awareness, social awareness, self-management, relationship skills,* and *responsible decision-making* categories (CASEL, 2020). I do this because I believe that, in order to redesign educational practices and to create antiracist activities, we must employ all SEL competencies, including *self-management,* by which we engage in self-care activities so that we do not burn out as we redesign our work. I believe that SEL is foundational to antiracist work in that we must become *self-aware* of the ways in which our thoughts and feelings about students of color make us respond to them, how our perceptions influence our decision-making during problem-solving team meetings, and how we set goals for students of color in the classroom; we must become *socially aware* of how our students respond to our presence, how they respond to the instruction we provide in the classroom, and how they respond to racially explicit content, including content that deems their racial group as inferior and backward people. We must also employ *relationship skills* to connect with allies in the field and build solidarity with individuals across race, class, culture, and gender in order to achieve equity goals. Finally, I believe that we must draw from the *responsible decision-making* competency such that we balance our work with theory and practice, rather than focusing solely on theory *or* practice. Therefore, CASEL's (2020) framework guides activities in the next section.

The following is a format of the activities. Each activity section starts with the *background*, which includes CASEL's (2020) SEL definitions. I adapt the definitions in culturally meaningful ways to use for each activity. Following the background, I state the *purpose* of the activity, the *objectives* for the activity, the *materials* you will need in order to engage with the activity, and what you will need to do to *prepare* for the activity. I include *theoretical context* for the activity, which provides context for the purpose of the activity, and *directions* which include the instructions for the activity. Finally, I include *workspace* at the end of each activity to provide space for you to document your thoughts and to complete the SEL activity.

Here is a visual of what you can expect:

SEL Competency: refers to the SEL competency for the activity

Background: defines the SEL competency for the activity

Purpose: states the aim and purpose of the activity

Objectives: states what you should expect to accomplish from the activity

Materials Needed: includes supplies you will need for the activity

Preparation: includes recommendations on how you can prepare for the activity

Theoretical Context for the Activity: provides a theoretical context for the activity

Directions: includes instructions on how to interact with the activity

Workspace: provides space for you to complete the SEL activity

Overview of SEL Activities

I. Self-Awareness Activities:

1.1   Your Racial-Cultural Journey Map

1.2   Reflection

1.3   Teacher Training Programs

1.4   Current Practices

II. Social Awareness Activities:

2.1   Engagement Among Students of Color

2.2   Student Perception of Racially Explicit Content

III. Self-Management Activities:

3.1   Activist Burnout

3.2   Designing Your Self-Care Plan

3.3   Racial Trauma

IV. Relationship Skills Activities:

4.1   Relationship Directory

V. Responsible Decision-Making Activities:

5.1   Resolving Current Challenges

Considering this is a work section, in which you will engage in reflective and writing activities, it is important that you have access to the physical copy of this book so that you can use the workspace to engage with the activities. If you are reading an online version of this book, I recommend that you purchase a notebook to use as your workspace. Although you can use separate sheets of paper to complete the activities, a notebook will keep all of your processing notes and activities together.

Now that you have some knowledge on what to expect, are you ready? Let's begin!

I. Self-Awareness Activities

"Know thyself."
~African Proverb

Background:
Self-awareness definition:

"The ability to accurately recognize one's own emotions, thoughts, and values and how they influence behavior" (CASEL, 2020, Competency section).

The following is a culturally adapted self-awareness definition to reference for activities in this section:

The ability to recognize the ways in which personal-historical, racial, and cultural experiences shape one's perceptions, attitudes, and beliefs concerning racial groups, including people of color.

The ability to recognize one's thoughts and feelings concerning antiracism and how those thoughts and emotions influence actions concerning antiracist education.

The ability to recognize one's thoughts and feelings concerning culturally sustaining pedagogy and how those thoughts and emotions influence actions concerning culturally sustaining pedagogy (see chapter three for a discussion on culturally sustaining pedagogy).

Activity 1.1: Your Racial-Cultural Journey Map

Purpose:

- To construct a racial-cultural journey map that illustrates your racial and cultural experiences.

Objectives:

By the end of this activity, you will

- reflect on racial and cultural events that have occurred throughout your development.
- illustrate a journey map of your lived experiences with race and culture.

Materials Needed:

- writing utensil
- workspace 1.1

Note: If you are reading an online version of this book, you'll need multiple sheets of paper to construct your racial-cultural journey map. Although you can use single sheets of paper, I recommend that you use a notebook so that you can compile your activities in one space.

Preparation:

1. Access the paper and writing utensil you will use to construct your racial-cultural journey map.
2. Find a quiet place to reflect on your lived experiences with race and culture.
3. If you enjoy listening to music as you reflect, feel free to play background music as you engage with this self-awareness activity. Take a moment to find your music of choice.

Theoretical Context for this Activity: Historicity

According to CHAT, we must examine current problems or concerns from a historical perspective in order to understand them (see chapter three for a discussion on CHAT). From this perspective, it is necessary to retrace our development and document racial experiences that have influenced our current ways of thinking in order to understand our beliefs and attitudes concerning antiracist education, racial equity work, and culturally sustaining practices. We must also retrace our history in order to examine how events throughout our development may influence how we perceive students of color, their cultures, languages, literacies, identities, and communities. Considering we learn through activities and employ cultural tools to accomplish tasks, activities in this section begin with creating a racial-cultural journey map that details your experiences with race and culture.

Directions:

Reflect on your racial and cultural experiences as far back as you can remember. Considering schooling is a racial and cultural experience, be sure to include on your map memories from teacher-training programs. I have included age ranges below to prompt your reflection. Consider significant events that have occurred in your life during each age range. You obviously may not be able to recall events from your early childhood experiences. However, if you've experienced traumatic events during your early childhood years, you may be able to recall them.

Play Age:	3-6 years old
School Age:	6-12 years old
Adolescence:	12-19 years old
Early Adulthood:	20-25 years old
Adulthood:	26-64 years old
Late Adulthood:	65+ years old

While it may be challenging to reflect on earlier age ranges, consider the following experiences and events in your lifetime:

- significant personal events, family events, and neighborhood experiences pertaining to race throughout your development.
- direct and subliminal messages you received, starting from early elementary school through undergraduate and graduate school about White people and people of color.
- significant racial and cultural societal events you have lived through (such as the civil rights movement, the war on poverty, race riots, and other racially motivated events, including the experiences of George Floyd, Breonna Taylor, and Ahmaud Arbery).
- beliefs your parents and relatives passed down to you concerning racial groups who are dissimilar from your racial group and narratives and lessons your parents taught you about people of color and White people.

Based on your developmental experiences, reflect on the racial and cultural events that have shaped your current perspective about race, social justice, and people of color. Be creative. You can either (1) draw *images* that represent events and experiences, (2) draw a *timeline* of your events and experiences, or (3) draw visual images *and* create a timeline that represents your racial and cultural events and experiences. Use as many pages as you need to illustrate your racial memories. Use workspace 1.1 on the next page to construct your journey map. When you finish your map, set aside time for deep breathing. Close your eyes. Inhale through your nose for four seconds and exhale through your mouth for four seconds. Do this at least 4 times and then conclude this activity.

Workspace 1.1:

Workspace 1.1 Continued:

Activity 1.2: Reflection

Purpose:
- To reflect on and document thoughts and emotions that emerged from constructing your racial-cultural journey map.

Objectives:
By the end of this activity, you will
- reflect on your lived experiences and racial memories, using your racial-cultural journey map.
- list thoughts and feelings that emerged from constructing your racial-cultural map.
- reflect on racial-cultural experiences and events throughout history that may contribute to current beliefs and attitudes concerning social justice, White people, people of color, and antiracist education.

Materials Needed:
- racial-cultural journey map
- writing utensil
- workspace 1.2

Note: If you are reading an online version of this book, you'll need multiple sheets of paper to list thoughts and feelings that emerged from constructing your racial-cultural journey map.

Preparation:
1. Access your racial-cultural journey map.
2. Find a quiet place to reflect on your racial-cultural journey map.
3. If you enjoy listening to music as you reflect, feel free to play background music as you engage with this self-awareness activity. Take a moment to find your music of choice.

Theoretical Context for this Activity: Thoughts, Feelings, and Behaviors
Cognitive behavioral psychological theories tell us that, in any given situation, our thoughts, feelings, and behaviors influence each other (Farmer, & Chapman,

2016). Although cognitive psychology and behavioral psychology were once competing theories, psychologists now integrate principles from the two camps in order to understand how our internal processes—such as thoughts, attitudes, and beliefs—are influenced by environmental factors. According to cognitive-behavioral principles, our thoughts and perceptions about people influence how we feel about and act toward them. Reflecting on our lived experiences with race and culture may bring to our consciousness experiences and events that make us feel a certain way. These feelings may influence the way we think about things, and our thoughts may influence our behaviors. Cognitive behavioral theories are often illustrated by the following triangle to demonstrate how our thoughts, feelings, and behaviors influence one another.

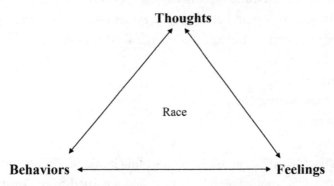

How we *think* affects how we act and feel.

Thoughts

Race

Behaviors ⟷ **Feelings**

How we *act* affects what we think and feel.   How we *feel* affects what we think and do.

Directions:

In workspace 1.2 below, document the thoughts and emotions your racial-cultural memories triggered. Consider the following questions as you reflect on racial memories and societal events you included on your map:

- What *thoughts* emerged from each age range as you reflected on racial and cultural memories? (see age ranges from Activity 1.1.)
- What *feelings* emerged in response to your thoughts?
- What did you do (behaviors) in response to your thoughts and emotions (i.e., did you share a thought or experience with a family or friend? Did you stop writing to reflect more deeply on your experiences? Were you moved to tears?)?
- In what ways might your racial and cultural experiences contribute to how you think and feel about antiracist education?
- In what ways might your lived experiences influence how you think and feel about students of color, their abilities, their literacies, and their languages?
- How might your thoughts and feelings about students of color affect how you teach them, set standards for them, and respond to their behaviors in the classroom?
- How might your racial and cultural history influence your perceptions concerning culturally sustaining teaching? (See chapter three for a discussion on culturally sustaining teaching.)

In the appropriate workspace charts below, document the thoughts and emotions that emerged from processing your racial-cultural journey map. In the last chart, document any behavioral responses that your thoughts and emotions influenced. Conclude this activity with deep breathing exercises.

Workspace 1.2:

***Thoughts* That Emerged While Processing Your Journey Map:**

Feelings That Emerged While Processing Your Journey Map:

Behaviors You Demonstrated While Processing Your Journey Map:

Activity 1.3: Teacher Training Programs

Purpose:

- To reflect on racial and cultural experiences that influenced your teaching philosophies and to determine how those philosophies currently influence how you provide instruction when working with students of color.

Objectives:

By the end of this activity, you will

- reflect on teacher training experiences.
- identify if your teacher training experiences have prepared you to create culturally sustaining, inclusive, and antiracist practices.

Materials Needed:

- writing utensil
- racial-cultural journey map
- workspace 1.3

Note: If you are reading an online version of this book, you'll need a notebook or multiple sheets of paper to document your thoughts concerning your teacher training experiences.

Preparation:

1. Access the paper and writing utensil you will use to document experiences with your teacher training program.
2. Find a quiet place to reflect on your teacher training experiences and current practices.
3. If you enjoy listening to music as you reflect, feel free to play background music as you engage with this self-awareness activity. Take a moment to find your music of choice.

Theoretical Context for This Activity: Deficit Thinking

Prior to and during the 1960s and 1970s, social scientists constructed racist theories to describe the underperformance of students of color and students who came from impoverished communities (Ryan, 1971). For example, scholars argued that students of color underperformed because of genetic and cultural deficits (Gould, 1996). Scholars contended that students of color and students from low socioeconomic backgrounds did not have the genetic makeup to perform well academically and that their languages, cultures, communities, and ways of being were deficient. Scholars argued that cultural deficiencies led to underperformance in the classroom. While many teachers now reject genetic explanations for underachievement, many embrace deficit theories, racist theories that attribute underperformance of students of color to students' cultures, languages, communities, and parents. While blaming students, educators who embrace deficit thinking may not examine racist school policies, norms, and practices that lead to student disengagement and underperformance.

Directions:
Reflect on your teacher training experiences. Use your journey map as a reference if you included teacher training experiences on your map. While you reflect, consider the theories and narratives that you read throughout your programs. As you reflect on your teacher training experiences, allow the following questions to guide your reflection. Use workspace 1.3 to share your responses:

- How did your teacher-training program prepare you for antiracist education and racial equity work?
- Did you learn about culturally relevant, responsive, and/or sustaining practices in your program or was your program steeped in Eurocentric theories and whiteness?
- Whether indirectly or directly, what did your teacher training program teach you about students of color, their cultures, their languages, their literacies, their parents, and their communities?
- What experiences influenced your current practices as a school-practitioner?
- How did theories, books, professors, and students describe students of color, their abilities, their languages, and their cultures?
- What reasons did theories, professors, and students provide in your cohort to explain the underperformance of students of color, and were those reasons influenced by racist, deficit thinking?
- How have deficit theories influenced your perspectives on teaching?

Document your thoughts in Workspace 1.3.

Workspace 1.3

Reflection: Teacher Training Experiences

Activity 1.4: Current Practices

Purpose:
- To reflect on current practices that empower both students of color and White students.

Objective:
By the end of this activity, you will
- list activities that sustain ethnic, racial, and cultural identities among students of color and White students.

Materials Needed:
- writing utensil
- workspace 1.4

Note: If you are reading an online version of this book, you'll need a sheet of paper to document your current practices.

Preparation:
1. Access the paper and writing utensil you will use to list your current practices.
2. Find a quiet place to reflect on and list your current practices.
3. If you enjoy listening to music as you reflect, feel free to play background music as you engage with this self-awareness activity. Take a moment to find your music of choice.

Theoretical Context for This Activity: Debunking White Normative Perspectives

Antiracist education requires practitioners to identify and reject current practices that oppress students of color. These include practices that might subliminally teach White students that they are superior to other racial group members, while teaching students of color that they are inferior to White students. As practitioners, we must disrupt the notion that Eurocentric values and ideologies are the standard by which all things should be measured.

Practitioners must resist White normative perspectives—"the often unconscious and invisible ideas and practices that make whiteness appear natural and right" (Ward, 2008, p. 563). White practitioners may be oblivious of how books and articles they use in the classroom strengthen ethnic, racial, and cultural identities among White students while oppressing students of color. Becoming an antiracist educator and redesigning practices in ways that are equitable require that practitioners become aware of how activities, posters, books, and articles may empower some students and depress others; stated differently, teacher-practitioners must become aware of how their curricula may strengthen the ethnic, racial, and cultural identities of White students while oppressing students of color.

Directions:

Reflect on your current classroom practices. Document the activities that you currently implement in your classroom that may strengthen ethnic, racial, and/or cultural identities among your students. This activity requires deep reflection; it considers White normative perspectives that practitioners may hold. For example, practitioners may perceive reading various American History books as "American history," without considering the impact the books have on students of color. While we must teach American history, we must include the contributions people of color and women have made to this country. When documenting current activities, consider your classroom rules and norms. Do they clash with the cultural values of students of color? Additionally, consider curricula content, language that you endorse and language that you correct during instructional time, and cultural *values* that you embrace and cultural *behaviors* that you punish. Which students do you empower through your actions? Complete the charts in the workspace below as you reflect on your classroom practices. Consider the following definitions as you complete the charts in the workspace below:

Racial ethnic identity "refers to a sense of group or collective identity based on one's perception that he or she shares a common heritage with a particular racial group" (Chavez & Guido-DiBrito, 1999, p. 40). *Cultural identity* "refers to an individual's sense of self derived from formal or informal membership in groups that transmit and inculcate knowledge, beliefs, values, attitudes, traditions, and ways of life" (Jameson, 2007, p. 199).

Workspace 1.4:

Activities and actions that may strengthen ethnic, racial, and cultural identity among White students:	In what ways might these activities strengthen ethnic, racial, and cultural identity among White students:

Activities and actions that may strengthen ethnic, racial, and cultural identity among youth of color:	In what ways might these activities strengthen ethnic, racial, and cultural identity among youth of color:

II. Social-Awareness Activities

"I am where I am because of the bridges that I crossed. Sojourner Truth was a bridge. Harriet Tubman was a bridge. Ida B. Wells was a bridge. Madame C. J. Walker was a bridge. Fannie Lou Hamer was a bridge."
~Oprah Winfrey

Background:
Social awareness definition:

"The ability to take the perspective of and empathize with others, including those from diverse backgrounds and cultures. The ability to understand social and ethical norms for behavior and to recognize family, school, and community resources and supports" (CASEL, 2020, Competency section).

The following is a culturally adapted social awareness definition to reference for activities in this section.

The ability to understand how racial and cultural experiences—including experiences during teacher training programs—influence your instructional practices in the classroom.

Activity 2.1: Engagement Among Students of Color

Purpose:
- To reflect on academic engagement among students of color.

Objective:
   By the end of this activity, you will
- become socially aware of how students of color engage with classroom activities.

Materials Needed:
- writing utensil
- workspace 2.1

Note: If you are reading an online version of this book, you'll need multiple sheets of paper to document activities you facilitate in the classroom.

Preparation:
1. Access the paper and writing utensil you will use to document your thoughts.
2. Find a quiet place to reflect on how students of color respond to instructional lessons and activities.
3. If you enjoy listening to music as you reflect, feel free to play background music as you engage with this social awareness activity. Take a moment to find your music of choice.

Theoretical Context for this Activity: Student Engagement
Scholars contend that practitioners can engage students in at least three different ways: behaviorally, emotionally, and cognitively (Fredricks, Blumenfeld, & Paris, 2004). *Behavioral* engagement refers to the extent to which individuals participate or involve themselves in an activity. *Emotional* engagement refers to emotional involvement by which students perceive activities as entertaining, rewarding, and meaningful. *Cognitive* engagement

refers to intellectual involvement in a particular activity, by which students actively reflect upon and produce ideas that contribute to the activity. How do students respond to your activities? Which students engage behaviorally (such as nodding their heads during instructional time), emotionally (such as showing excitement about the activity), and/or cognitively (such as involving themselves in deep reflection and processing of information)? Decades of research show that students tend to engage at a high level when practitioners design culturally meaningful activities in the classroom, whereas students may disengage when instruction is unrelated to their cultures, experiences, and interests.

Directions:

In the workspace below, document activities that typically produce behavioral, emotional, and cognitive engagement among culturally diverse learners. While there is certainly variability in the ways in which students prefer to learn during instructional time, the purpose of this activity is to become aware of the activities that have been effective at engaging students of color in your classroom. You might find that the activities that have been effective at engaging students of color are the same activities that have been effective at engaging the majority of your students. Document these activities in the charts below. In the reflection section below, reflect on how these activities may be culturally sustaining for students; that is, consider how the activities sustain, perpetuate, and foster the cultures, languages, and identities of students of color.

Workspace 2.1

List Behaviorally Engaging Activities in This Chart:

List Emotionally Engaging Activities in This Chart:

List Cognitively Engaging Activities in This Chart:

Reflection:

In What Ways are the Above Activities Culturally Sustaining?

Activity 2.2: Student Perception of Racially Explicit Content

Purpose:
- To recognize how students of color respond to curricula that explicitly address race and culture, including educational materials that reference the n-word.

Objective:
By the end of this activity, you will
- become socially aware of how your students respond to racially explicit content, including text that reference the "n-word" and audio resources that vocalize the word.

Materials Needed:
- writing utensil
- workspace 2.2

Note: If you are reading an online version of this book, you'll need multiple sheets of paper to reflect on student perception of racially explicit content.

Preparation:
1. Access the paper and writing utensil for this activity.
2. Find a quiet place to reflect on how your students respond to racially explicit content.
3. If you enjoy listening to music as you reflect, feel free to play background music as you engage with this social awareness activity. Take a moment to find your music of choice.

Theoretical Context for this Activity: Racially Explicit Content and Student Responses

Cultural historical activity theory (CHAT) contends that individuals learn, develop, engage, and establish relationships through activities. All instructional practices that practitioners employ in the classroom are rooted in culture. In my years of practicing as a school psychologist, I have worked with students of color who lamented that they disliked certain teachers and avoided their classes. Over the years, students have stated, "Mr. Williams, I am so tired of reading books about slavery, books about oppressing Black people, and books that include the word nigger." Others have stated, "I hate being the only Black person in the classroom when we read books that include the n-word." Over the years, students have expressed distress and frustration about "spending Black History Month revisiting slavery" and reading books like *To Kill a Mockingbird* throughout the semester. Students have shared experiences of their teachers and peers reading the n-word from articles and books. They have also shared experiences of teachers using audio recordings in class that use the n-word. Students addressed how they experience social and emotional distress from these experiences; they've shared that they have purposefully gotten themselves removed from class by engaging in disruptive behaviors or that they have skipped class to avoid the stress that comes with racially explicit content.

Directions:

Reflect on how your students of color respond to activities that reference the n-word and activities that explicitly address race in your classroom (or within your school building if you don't share racially explicit content in your classroom). In the workspace below, document any experiences in which students of color have articulated how they feel about curricula that reference slavery, the n-word, or being made to feel racially inferior in the classroom. Reflect on how you prepare your students for historical events that reference slavery and oppression of group members. As you reflect, consider the following questions:

- In what ways can I provide culturally sustaining, inclusive, and equitable practices when teaching American history or sharing racialized content?
- How do I respond to my students' feedback when they share how racialized content makes them feel?

If you are not a classroom teacher and do not read books and narratives in the classroom concerning race and culture, reflect on the experiences that students of color have shared with you about the books they read in class that portray people of color as inferior to White people. How do you respond to their feedback? In what ways can you empower them as youth of color?

Use the workspace below to share your thoughts.

Workspace 2.2:

III. Self-Management Activities

"In the midst of movement and chaos keep stillness inside of you."
~Deepak Chopra

Background:

Self-management definition:

"The ability to successfully regulate one's emotions, thoughts, and behaviors in different situations—effectively managing stress, controlling impulses, and motivating oneself. The ability to set and work toward personal and academic goals" (CASEL, 2020, Competency section).

The following are culturally adapted self-management definitions to reference for activities in this section.

The ability to use culturally meaningful management strategies when engaging in racial, cultural, and equity work. (I describe culturally meaningful strategies as self-management strategies that we all have learned from our cultural groups. These might include self-talk, praying, meditating, processing stress and trauma using music, connecting with others in solidarity, and so on.)

The ability to manage oneself when experiencing stress, tension, and anxiety as a result of racial, cultural, and equity work.

The ability to continue racial, cultural, and equity work when feeling frustrated, exhausted, and ineffective.

Activity 3.1: Activist Burnout

Purpose:

To define and discuss activist burnout.

Objectives:

By the end of this activity, you will

- recognize the meaning of activist burnout.
- list stress related symptoms you experience when engaging with antiracist work.
- recognize self-management strategies you currently employ to de-stress when engaging with antiracist work.

Materials Needed:

- writing utensil
- workspace 3.1

Note: If you are reading an online version of this book, you'll need multiple sheets of paper to document how you experience stress and trauma when engaging with racial equity work.

Preparation:

1. Access the paper and writing utensil you will use to list stress related symptoms you experience when engaging with antiracist work.
2. Find a quiet place to reflect on the notion of activist burnout.
3. If you enjoy listening to music as you reflect and document, feel free to play background music as you engage with this self-management activity. Take a moment to find your music of choice.

Theoretical Context for this Activity: Activist Burnout

Engaging in antiracist work renders practitioners susceptible to a tremendous amount of stress, which could lead to physical and mental exhaustion. According to social movement scholars, "activist burn out"—which occurs when "the accumulation of stressors associated with activism become so overwhelming they compromise activists' persistence in their activism" (Gorski, 2019, p. 667)—

is among the most formidable barriers to realizing change (Cox, 2011; Pigni, 2016). According to Noushad (2008), the term burnout was first used in the novel *A Burnt-Out Case* (Green, 1961), which depicted the life of an architect who was exhausted from work to the extent that he became unmotivated and could neither "suffer nor laugh" (as cited in Noushad, 2008, p. 1). Psychologist and author Herbert J. Freudenberger introduced the term burnout into the academic literature in 1974 and defined it as "to fail, to wear out, or become exhausted by making excessive demands on energy, strength, or resources" (Freudenberger, 1974, p. 159). He perceived burnout as a long-term condition that is more debilitating than temporary fatigue (Gorski & Chen, 2015). Since Freudenberger's conception of burnout, other scholars have elaborated on his definition.

Other definitions of burnout include: "a state of exhaustion" (Schaufeli & Buunk, 2003, p. 383); "the end result of a process in which idealistic and highly committed people lose their spirit" (Pines, 1994, p. 381); "the deterioration of the wellbeing of activists resulting in the deterioration of social justice movements" (as cited in Gorski & Erakat, 20019, p. 785). In a study titled *Fighting Racism, Battling Burnout: Causes of Activist Burnout in US Racial Justice Activists*, Gorski (2019) described the experiences of thirty racial justice activists who all experienced burnout. While activists experienced a host of concerns that resulted in stress, twenty-nine out of thirty of them revealed that emotional causes resulted in burnout. In a different study, Chen and Gorski (2015) found that, of the twenty-two activists who shared their experiences with social justice and human rights activism, all had experienced some level of burnout to which they discontinued their activism and sought emotional support; after caring for themselves, they returned to activism. Considering the intense involvement in challenging racist policies and practices, antiracist practitioners may benefit from documenting their experiences with stress in order to best prepare for self-care plans (see Activity 3.2 for self-care plans) as a preventive method to burnout.

Directions:

In the chart below, document your experiences with tension, stress, and anxiety when engaging with racial, cultural, and equity work. In the *middle column,* record what your physical symptoms feel like when engaging with racial, cultural, and equity work. In the left column, determine whether you believe the feeling is associated with tension, anxiety, stress or other factors when engaging with the work. In the *right column*, share how you manage physical symptoms.

Workspace 3.1

Anxiety/Tension/ Stress/Other	Physical Symptom(s)	Stress Management

Activity 3.2: Designing Your Self-Care Plan

Purpose:
- To design your self-care plan.

Objective:
By the end of this activity, you will
- design a self-care plan to prepare for stress that you may experience as you engage with antiracist work.

Materials Needed:
- writing utensil
- workspace 3.2

Note: If you are reading an online version of this book, you'll need multiple sheets of paper to design your self-care plan.

Preparation:
1. Access the paper and writing utensil you will use to create your self-care plan.
2. Find a quiet place to construct your plan.
3. If you enjoy listening to music as you design your self-care plan, feel free to play background music as you engage with this self-management activity. Take a moment to find your music of choice.

Theoretical Context for this Activity: Self-Care Plan

Considering the research on activist burnout (Freudenberger, 1974; Gorski & Chen, 2015; Gorski, 2019; Gorski & Erakat, 2019), practitioners may benefit from identifying and utilizing self-care and self-management strategies as preventive measures when addressing race, culture, and equity; educators may benefit from having knowledge of stress reduction techniques and engaging with self-care activities when experiencing tension, stress, frustration, and anxiety resulting from antiracist work and when challenging the status quo. Self-care refers to individuals making informed decisions about their wellbeing and health (Omisakin & Ncama, 2011); it includes all activities that we engage with to care for our physical, emotional, spiritual, and social self. Self-management, on the other hand, is the ability to regulate thoughts, emotions, and behaviors (CASEL, 2020). Therefore, while self-care includes a repertoire of activities that we engage with to care for ourselves, self-management refers to abilities and require training. However, engaging in continual self-care activities may reduce stress, make managing oneself easier when experiencing stressful events, and reduce the potential for activist burnout.

Considering racial equity work requires self-care activities as methods to prevent burnout, activities in this section include creating *culturally sustaining self-care plans*. Remember, "culturally sustaining" refers to the idea of fostering, perpetuating, and sustaining cultural ways of being (Paris, 2012, p. 93). Although practitioners have a tendency to "teach" self-care activities, we all have culturally meaningful ways that we de-stress. For example, attending religious and spiritual services, listening to music, gathering with family and friends, self-communing, meditating, dancing, reading, writing, and praying are a few culturally meaningful self-care activities that we learn from cultural group members. Believing that individuals do not have effective ways to de-stress is an example of deficit thinking. It may be more appropriate to say individuals do not engage with self-care strategies they've learned overtime or that they have adopted self-care habits that are self-defeating rather than self-liberating. Additionally, while cultural group members have self-care strategies they use to de-stress, they may not have knowledge of the importance of creating a self-care plan and the benefits of following that plan. Often, social service practitioners ignore the ways that cultural group members use cultural assets and cultural tools to cope with stress. Rather than drawing from the assets of students of color, practitioners often teach strategies they learn from training programs, articles, and books. In this section, we will identify culturally meaningful strategies that we employ to de-stress; we will seek to sustain those strategies by acknowledging them, adding to them, and inserting them into our self-care plans. A self-care plan is "a thoughtful constructed and intentionally engaged guide to promote our health and wellbeing" (*Marshfield Clinic Division of Education*, 2020, Self-care Section).

Directions:

We will create a self-care plan in four steps.

Step 1:

In the workspace below, document positive self-care activities you currently employ throughout the week or when dealing with stress. Positive activities that I engage with include praying, reading the Bible and other inspirational texts, attending church services, listening to music—including gospel, rap, R&B, and jazz—communing with family and friends, and connecting with affinity groups. While I currently engage with the aforementioned activities, and while those activities are culturally meaningful for me, I also de-stress by writing, meditating, and working out. Considering we may employ positive and/or negative coping strategies when we are stressed, be sure to document negative strategies you use that may hinder self-care goals. I'll call negative coping strategies "self-defeating" behaviors. These include isolating yourself, overworking, "stress-related eating," gossiping, and other self-defeating activities. In the workspace below, document positive coping activities and self-defeating behaviors that you demonstrate when you are stressed.

Workspace 3.2

Positive Activities	Self-Defeating Behaviors

Step 2:

Next, based on the positive activities and self-defeating behaviors you've documented above, categorize your positive activities in the spaces below based on *physical* self-care, *mental* self-care, *emotional* self-care, *social* self-care, and *spiritual* self-care. The purpose of categorizing your activities is to collect data on your self-care activities and to identify which areas of self-care you pay attention to most. Categorize your positive activities in the spaces below.

The following are examples of self-care activities you may include:

- **Physical Care:** sleeping, healthy eating, cardio and weight training activities.
- **Mental Care:** journaling, reading, writing, entertaining activities (puzzles, movies, games and so on).
- **Emotional Care:** meditation/yoga, listening to music, processing feelings with family, friends, and affinity group members, counseling or life coaching activities.
- **Social Care:** connecting with family and friends, social outings with family, friends, and affinity group members, and activities that lead to forming deeper relationships with colleagues who are dedicated to antiracist work.
- **Spiritual Care:** attending worship services, connecting with spiritual leaders, listening to spiritual music, praying, reading spiritual literature, meditating, connecting with nature, and other activities.

Categorize the self-care activities you currently engage with throughout the week:

Physical Care:	Mental Care:	Emotional Care:	Social Care:	Spiritual Care:

Step 3:

In the chart below, I have included additional examples of self-care activities for each self-care category. Now that you have categorized your self-care activities in Step 2, circle the activities in the chart below that you'd consider including within your self-care plan.

Physical Care:	Mental Care:	Emotional Care:	Social Care:	Spiritual Care:
Sufficient sleep	Movie night	Meditation /	Connect with	Engage in
Create sleep	w/ family	Mindfulness	colleagues	spiritual
routine	Game night	Adult coloring	outside of	worship
Nutritional eating	w/ family	books	work	(singing,
Medical checkups	Reading	Read positive	Host a	dancing, etc)
Take lunch breaks	Writing	quotes	gathering at	Make time
Use sick leave/	Professional	Treat yourself	your home	to attend
time	development	Develop SEL	Create time	services
Use mental sick	Avoid toxic	competencies	to learn more	Watch online
leave	people	Engage in	about your	services
Exercise before &	Piece together	positive self-	colleagues	Read spiritual
after work at least	puzzles	talk	Share personal	quotes
3 times a week	Practice	Watch comedy	narratives with	Forgive
Get a massage	saying no	clips	colleagues	yourself
Take pride in	Say yes to the	Find time for	Create affinity	Forgive others
appearance:	things you	music, dancing,	groups	Let go of the
grooming and	want	and laughter	Establish	things that
clothing, etc	Read daily	Practice a	workout	hurt you
Walk outdoors	affirmations	new breathing	partners	
Stretch	Reflect	technique		
Take naps	on daily	Allow yourself		
	affirmations	to look forward		
	Read	to events and		
	inspirational	activities		
	quotes	Create time for		
	Reflect on	silence		
	inspirational	Create a		
	quotes	playlist of your		
		favorite songs		

See Thrive Global (2018, 53 Powerful self-care ideas) for more activities

Step 4:

Now that you have organized activities into self-care categories, select 1-2 activities from each category (from Step 2 and Step 3) to construct your self-care plan below. Be sure to select 1-2 activities that you can engage with daily or weekly within each category. Also, be sure to select specific, measurable, attainable, realistic, and time-bound activities from Step 2 and Step 3 (Marshfield Clinic, 2020, Self-Care Plans Section). I have created a self-care plan that I will follow based on the items in Step 3 to provide an example for you. I have selected 1-2 activities from each self-care category that are specific, measurable, attainable, realistic, and time-bound. Notice that my self-care plan is based on my work schedule: *before* work, *during* work, and *after* work activities. Let's use the "physical activities" I will engage with *before work* as an example from the chart below. The activities are *specific* (deep breathing and riding stationary bike); they are *measurable* (breathing activity for 5 minutes and bike riding for 20 minutes); they are *attainable* for me considering I wake up an hour and a half prior to leaving for work, I have a stationary bike in my home office, and I can fit both activities into my morning schedule; they are *realistic* in that I have access to the bike and typically ride it 40 minutes a day, and I can engage in deep breathing upon waking in the morning; the activities are time-bound in that they have a starting and ending time. Review my before work, during work, and after work self-care plans, then, in the space below, select 1-2 activities from each self-care category (Step 2 and Step 3) to create your self-care plan.

My Self-Care Plan *Before* Work:

Physical	Mental	Emotional	Social	Spiritual
1. Upon waking, engage in deep breathing for 5 minutes. 2. Ride stationary bike for 20 minutes.	1. Read daily proverb (1 minute). 2. State aloud an affirmation on how my day will go (10 seconds).	1. Mediate upon waking (5 minutes while breathing deeply). 2. Listen to music playlist while driving into work (30 minutes).	1. Wish my family a good day and hug them prior to leaving for work (1 minute). 2. Kiss my daughter and wife and give my son dap on my way out of the house (1 minute).	1. Read Proverbs (2 minutes). 2. Pray daily proverb (self-talk).

See Marshfield Clinic (2020) for additional information on constructing self-care plans.

My Self-Care Plan *During* Work:

Physical	Mental	Emotional	Social	Spiritual
1. Use the stairs throughout the day rather than the elevator (from 8:00am – 3:15pm).	1. Reflect on daily proverb (during first passing period – 4 minutes).	1. Play background music in my office throughout the day while working.	1. Greet my colleagues by name and ask them how their day is going.	1. Recite affirmations from daily proverb during three different passing periods.

My Self-Care Plan *After* Work:

Physical	Mental	Emotional	Social	Spiritual
1. Eat a healthy dinner mindfully with my family at least 3 hours before bed. 2. Go to bed at a set time and early enough to get 8 hours of sleep.	1. While in bed, reflect on my self-care plan for the day for five minutes.	1. Complete deep breathing while lying in bed for five minutes.	1. Spend first 15 minutes of my time in the house conversing with family about their day before doing anything else.	1. End the night with a 5-10 minute prayer with my family, thanking God for being with us throughout the day.

Construct your self-care plan below. Create your own title for each self-care plan and fill in the columns:

Title:

Physical	Mental	Emotional	Social	Spiritual

Title:

Physical	Mental	Emotional	Social	Spiritual

Title:

Physical	Mental	Emotional	Social	Spiritual

Now that you have created your self-care plan, create a schedule on when you will follow the plan.

Activity 3.3: Racial Trauma

Purpose:
- To understand racial trauma and its symptoms.

Objectives:
By the end of this activity, you will
- recognize the meaning of racial trauma.
- list symptoms associated with racial trauma.

Materials Needed:
- writing utensil
- workspace 3.3

Note: If you are reading an online version of this book, you'll need multiple sheets of paper to list racially traumatizing events you have experienced in your life.

Preparation:
1. Access the paper and writing utensil you will use for this activity.
2. Find a quiet place to reflect on and document symptoms associated with racial trauma.
3. If you enjoy listening to music as you reflect and document, feel free to play background music as you engage with this self-management activity. Take a moment to find your music of choice.

Theoretical Context for this Activity: Racial Trauma
When considering racial equity work, it is important that practitioners understand "racial trauma" (Comas-Díaz, Hall, & Neville, 2019, p. 1) and its symptoms; practitioners must have knowledge on how to respond when they feel they are reliving experiences of racial trauma. *Racial trauma* is a form of race-based stress and refers to "People of Color and Indigenous individuals' (POCI) reactions to dangerous events and real or perceived experiences of racial discrimination (p. 1) . . . [T]hese include threats of harm and injury, humiliating and shaming events, and witnessing harm to other POCI due to

real or perceived racism" (as cited in Comas-Diaz, Hall, & Neville, 2019, p. 1). While POCI may re-experience racial trauma as they engage with racial equity work, it is important that they know how to identify the trauma and have in their self-care plans tools and activities to deal with it. White colleagues are not exempt from experiencing trauma as they engage with racial equity work. I have worked with White colleagues who have shared traumatic events that they had experienced, and their trauma made them sensitive to race and gender. For example, a colleague of mine once shared an experience with race from her journey map and explained that, when she sees tall Black youth, she thinks about the experience she had with a tall Black male (see Introduction: *Racial Trauma* to read about my colleague's experience). Therefore, as racial equity practitioners, we must allocate sufficient time to address trauma, tension, stress, and anxiety when redesigning educational practices and preparing for antiracist education. Scholars have documented a host of symptoms that people of color may experience after encountering racial trauma (Comas-Diaz et al., 2019, p. 1), including the following:

- fear,
- hypervigilance,
- somatization,
- intrusive thoughts,
- headaches,
- insomnia,
- body aches,
- memory difficulty,
- self-blame,
- confusion,
- shame,
- guilt,
- depression after experiencing racism, and more.

Considering POCI engage in intense racial equity work, it is possible for them to relive traumatic events. Therefore, we must become aware of our experiences and include in our self-care plans activities that will help us process and cope with trauma so that we do not burnout and discontinue the work. To do this, practitioners can employ the substance abuse and mental health services administration's (SAMHSA, 2014) framework to think through their racially traumatizing experiences. When I discuss trauma with parents, students, and educators, I like to refer to SAMHSA's (2014) "three E's of trauma" (p. 8). According to SAMHSA (2014), "Individual trauma results from an ***event***, series of events, or set of circumstances that is ***experienced*** by an individual as physically or emotionally harmful or life threatening and that has lasting adverse ***effects*** on the individual's functioning and mental, physical, social, emotional, or spiritual well-being" (p. 7). One example of the three Es that I hear people of color articulate is their encounter with police officers. From witnessing the *events* of racial profiling and police brutality, many people of color explain that they *experience* tension, anxiety, and paranoia when they see or are pulled over by officers; they explain that it is challenging to manage emotions when encountering officers or seeing officers drive behind them, which has a lasting and disruptive—adverse—*effect* on their lives. According to SAMHSA's (2014) definition, an event is traumatic when it has a lasting effect on the lives of individuals.

Directions:

Using the charts below, document your racially traumatizing (1) *events* (3.3a), your *experiences* to those events (3.3b), and the *effects* of those events (3.3c). Refer to the example above (of how some people of color respond to the police) to understand *events*, *experiences*, and *effects*. If you've experienced racially traumatic events at some point in life, return to your self-care plan (Activity 3.2) and include activities that will help you process those experiences. Also, refer to your racial journey map (Activity 1.1) to identify racially traumatic experiences as you complete the charts below.

3.3a Racially Traumatic Event(s) (What Happened?):
1.
2.
3.
4.
5.

3.3b Experience(s) to Those Events (How you Responded):
1.
2.
3.
4.
5.

3.3c Effect(s) of Those Events (Duration of Stress):
1.
2.
3.
4.
5.

Prior to concluding this activity, take time to breathe deeply.

IV. Relationship Skills Activities

"You don't fight racism with racism, the best way
to fight racism is with solidarity."
~Bobby Seale

Background:
Relationship skills definition:

"The ability to establish and maintain healthy and rewarding relationships with diverse individuals and groups" (CASEL, 2020, Competency section).

The following is a culturally adapted relationship skills definition to reference for activities in this section:

The ability to establish and maintain positive relationships with culturally and racially diverse people, including students, parents, and community members in order to honor and learn from their rich histories, experiences, cultures, literacies, languages, and identities.

Activity 4.1: Relationship Directory

Purpose:
- To construct a relationship directory, which I define as a contact list of individuals you can establish relationships with in order to form accountability partners.

Objectives:
By the end of this activity, you will
- create a relationship directory—names of colleagues who are engaging with antiracist work.
- identify individuals to form racial equity accountability partners— partners who coach each other toward meeting goals—you can add to your "social" self-care plan.
- identify individuals to create affinity groups, which are groups of people who have common goals and interests.

Materials Needed:
- writing utensil
- workspace 4.1

Note: If you are reading an online version of this book, you'll need multiple sheets of paper to complete the relationship directory activity in this section.

Preparation:
1. Access the paper and writing utensil you will use to construct your relationship directory.
2. Find a quiet place to document names of potential accountability partners.
3. If you enjoy listening to music as you identify partners, feel free to play background music as you engage with this relationship skills activity. Take a moment to find your music of choice.

Theoretical Context for this Activity: Solidarity
Racial justice work requires building relationships with allies and working in solidarity with others across race, class, and gender. Generally, solidarity

refers to "a kind of connection to other people . . . to other members of a group" (Laitinen & Pessi, 2014, p. 2). When engaging with racial, cultural, and equity work, critical questions include the following:

- Who are allies committed to the cause you seek to improve?
- What can you learn from them?
- How can you contribute to their work?
- How can you support them?
- Who do you work well with?
- Who don't you work well with?
- Why don't you work well with those individuals?

Solidarity with other committed individuals is the force that leads to change; without it, efforts disintegrate (Heyed, 2007).

Directions:
In an effort to build a network of relationships to establish accountability partners and affinity groups, identify individuals who are engaging with racial equity work, individuals you are willing to connect and process with. Who will you connect and build solidarity with as you redesign your work and create change? Document their names in the chart below. Once you have documented their names, contact them to request forming accountability bonds while engaging with racial equity work. When speaking with colleagues you feel might be a suitable fit, share this activity with them and ask if they will be your accountability partner. Partners will encourage each other, provide strategies and feedback for each other, and check on each other throughout the week. Once you establish your accountability partners and affinity groups, include these in your self-care plans within the social care column, as interacting with accountability partners and affinity groups may reduce stress and the tendency to burnout overtime.

Workspace 4.1

Relationship Directory				
Name	**District**	**Title**	**Phone #**	**Email**

V. Responsible Decision-Making Activities

"Every social justice movement that I know of has come out of people sitting in small groups, telling their life stories, and discovering that other people have shared similar experiences."

~ Gloria Steinem

Background:

Responsible decision-making definition:

"The ability to make constructive choices about personal behavior and social interactions based on ethical standards, safety concerns, and social norms" (CASEL, 2020, Competency section).

The following is a culturally adapted responsible decision-making definition to reference for activities in this section:

The ability to engage in responsible, collaborative actions with people across race in order to design culturally responsive, inclusive, and antiracist practices.

Activity 5.1: Resolving Current Challenges

Purpose:
- To share an opportunity to collaborate with other educators who are reading this book, redesigning educational practices, and engaging with antiracist work.

Objectives:
By the end of this session, you will
- recognize the importance of interacting in community of practice support groups in order to enhance your racial equity work and as a social self-care activity.
- recognize the purpose of the *Redesign* and *Like Music* to My *Ears* Facebook groups as online social media community of practice supports.

Materials Needed:
- Phone/computer to access social media

Theoretical Context for this Activity: Research and Practice
Research shows that, while practitioners desire to create culturally responsive and sustaining practices, they have no clue where to start in the process (Samuels, 2018; Samuels, Samuels, & Cook, 2017). Scholars also show that practitioners struggle to implement culturally responsive and sustaining theories in the classroom. Based on these concerns, I have established the *Redesign* and *Like Music to My Ears* Facebook groups to offer support and coaching for practitioners, administrators, parents, and community leaders who are reading this book. The Facebook groups will provide additional coaching opportunities for practitioners who completed the activities in this book. In this section, you will document the challenges you are currently experiencing with redesigning your work. When you join the Facebook groups, you'll have the opportunity to access support to resolve the challenges you identify below.

Directions:

In the workspace below, document the challenges you are currently experiencing when designing culturally sustaining, inclusive, and antiracist practices. Once you document the concerns you continue to experience, join our *Redesign* Facebook group to get direct coaching from our team of consultants who are working to redesign educational practices in their classrooms. Consultants within our Facebook coaching groups are practitioners and administrators who are currently working at the ground level with students. In addition to receiving coaching from them, you'll receive direct coaching from me, as I will demonstrate how to redesign your practices. I will guide you through the process of illustrating your current practices on paper and show you exactly how to start making adjustments to your instructional lessons. If you are interested in receiving direct coaching on how to integrate hip-hop cultural elements with instruction in your classroom, counseling groups, or restorative justice circles, join our *Like Music to My Ears* Facebook group, where I will coach you on how to do it. In the workspace below, document the challenges you are currently experiencing when designing culturally sustaining activities. Conclude this activity by reflecting on your experiences using SEL competencies as a guiding framework to address race, culture, and antiracism—the first steps in the redesign process.

Workspace 5.1:

Current Challenges to Designing Equitable Practices:

Current Challenges to Designing Equitable Practices:

Thoughts on Using SEL as a First Step to Redesigning Practices:

Next Step?

Congratulations on taking the first step to work redesign! Again, the first step in redesigning your work to create culturally sustaining, inclusive, and antiracist practices begins with reflection. The next step requires redesigning instructional programming and activities. Connect with me in order to continue the conversation and to access additional strategies on how to redesign your work. The purpose of this book is to prepare you for work redesign. Unfortunately, educators who desire to implement equitable practices attempt to start with applying interventions in the classroom to fix their students when, often, the problem is the mindset of the educator. Culturally responsive, sustaining, and antiracist teaching begins with reflecting on our beliefs, attitudes, and experiences, and understanding how racial and cultural events, from a personal and historical perspective, have shaped our worldviews, ways of being, and ways of delivering instruction. Therefore, purchasing new programs to implement when redesigning work is never the first step. I wrote this book as a practical guide to help you with this process. This reflection journey is never ending. Although reflection never ends, we must not wait to act. We must act now. We must learn how to design or redesign curricula that employ the cultural literacies, languages, and lived experiences of students in order to create equitable experiences and opportunities in the classroom.

Here is how you can continue your journey.

Subscribe to My YouTube Channel
Subscribe to my YouTube channel, where I will provide direct coaching, using a white board in order to show you exactly how to design or redesign your classroom practices. While I use culturally responsive and sustaining theories and practices, I will use cultural historical activity theory (CHAT) to help you illustrate your practices in a concrete manner (on paper and on my white board) so that you can see your practices visually and analyze the cultural tools, rules, and norms you use to implement instructional activities. I will do this at my YouTube channel.

Redesign Facebook Group

Join our *Redesign An SEL Toolkit* community of practice Facebook group. Our community of practice group involves learning to design or redesign classroom practices. The goal of this group is to connect with parents, community leaders, practitioners, and administrators across race and culture in order to learn how to design culturally sustaining, inclusive, and antiracist classroom-based and organizational practices.

Like Music to My Ears Facebook Group

Join our *Like Music to My Ears* community of practice Facebook group. *Like Music to My Ears* involves learning to employ hip-hop elements including rap, dance, and the arts, when delivering social emotional learning and trauma informed supports in schools. From this group you will learn activities that you can share with students who embrace hip-hop. You will learn community building activities you can use in any class and with any subject.

I look forward to connecting with you and continuing the process of redesigning school-based practices in ways that are culturally sustaining, inclusive, and equitable for all learners.

Terms to Know When Considering Educational Equity Work

Affinity groups: individuals who are connected by a shared interest or passion and "who work together to develop skills that allow them to solve the particular sorts of problems that matter to the group[s]" (Gee, 2018, p. 8).

Affinity spaces: "loosely organized social and cultural settings in which the work of teaching tends to be shared by many people, in many locations, who are connected by a shared interest or passion" (Gee, 2018, p. 8).

Ally: "dominant group members who work to end prejudice in their personal and professional lives, and relinquish social privileges conferred by their group status through their support of nondominant groups" (as cited in Brown & Ostrove, 2013, p. 1).

Antiracist: "one who is supporting an antiracist policy through their actions or expressing an antiracist idea" (Kendi, 2019, p. 13).

Antiracist education: a term that describes the process of "[eliminating] institutionalized racism from the school and society and to help individuals to develop nonracist attitudes" (Banks & Banks, 1993, p. 357).

Cultural competence: "the ability to effectively provide services cross-culturally" (Diller, 2007, p. 310).

Cultural determinism: "the belief that if one student is designated as a member of a given cultural population, he or she must necessarily act or feel certain ways" (Boykin & Noguera, 2011, p. 97).

Cultural identity: "the process of adopting the beliefs and practices—the custom complexes—of one or more cultural communities" (as cited in Arnette, 2003, p. 286).

Cultural racism: "the belief that the cultural ways of one group are superior to those of another" (Diller, 2007, p. 2007).

Culturally relevant teaching: embodies an array of instructional practices that acknowledge and infuse the cultures of students with school curricula. Although theorists define culturally relevant teaching differently (Ladson-Billings, 1995; Gay, 2018, among others), it is a process of infusing the cultures and lived experiences of students with instruction. Culturally *relevant* teaching is also known as culturally *responsive* teaching (Gay, 2018).

Culturally responsive pedagogy: an umbrella term that refers to decades of theories and practices that utilize the cultures and assets of students as bridges to teach mainstream content (Gay, 2018).

Culturally sustaining pedagogy: rather than using the cultures of students of color to make mainstream content *relevant* and *responsive* to the lives of students, culturally sustaining pedagogy attempts to go a step further by perpetuating and fostering the languages, literacies, and identities of students (Paris, 2012). Essentially, CSP seeks to provide instruction that *sustains* the cultures, languages, and literacies of students. Ladson-Billings (2014) argues that CSP is a needed remix of her culturally relevant theory.

Culture: "the conscious and unconscious content that a group learns, shares, and transmits from generation to generation that organizes life and helps interpret existence" (Diller, 2007, p. 310); "it involves every aspect of the human endeavor" (Ladson-Billings, 2006, p. 143).

Deficit theories: "theories that situate school failure in the minds, bodies, communities and cultures of students" (Dudley-Marling, 2015, p. 1). "The goal of deficit approaches was to eradicate the linguistic, literate, and cultural practices many students of color brought from their homes and communities and to replace them with what were viewed as superior practices" (Paris, 2012, p. 93).

Educational equity: "an educational system where every student has access to the resources and educational rigor they need at the right moment in their education, irrespective of race, ethnicity, gender, sexual orientation, language, disability, family background, family income, citizenship, or tribal status" (Aspen Institute, 2018, p. 1).

Essentialism: "the belief that people have underlying, unchanging qualities that are their essence or their nature" (Boykin & Noguera, 2011, p. 97).

Ethnocentrism: "assessing, interpreting, and judging culturally different behavior in relation to one's own cultural standards. Such behaviors are acceptable to the extent that they are similar to one's own cultural ways" (Diller, 2007, p. 310).

Individual racism: "the beliefs, attitudes, and actions of individuals that support or perpetuate racism" (Wijeyesinghe et al., 1997, p. 89).

Inclusive: refers to "a continuous struggle toward (a) the redistribution of quality opportunities to learn and participate in educational programs, (b) the recognition and value of differences as reflected in content, pedagogy, and assessment tools, and (c) the opportunities for marginalized groups to represent themselves in decision-making processes that advance and define claims of exclusion and the respective solutions that affect their children's educational futures" (Waitoller & Kozleski, 2013, p. 35).

Institutional racism: "the manipulation of social institutions to give preference and advantages to Whites and at the same time restrict the choices, rights, mobility, and access of People of Color" (Diller, 2007, p. 310).

Justice: "an inner sense of fairness that requires retribution for wrongs done to self, other individuals, or groups including one's people" (Diller, 2007, p. 310).

Race: "refers to the attempt by physical anthropologists to divide human groups according to their physical traits and characteristics" (Banks, p. 359).

Racial equity: "the condition that would be achieved if one's racial identity no longer predicted, in a statistical sense, how one fares. This includes elimination of policies, practices, attitudes and cultural messages that reinforce differential outcomes by race or fail to eliminate them" (NRDC, 2019, p. 3).

Racial ethnic identity: "refers to a sense of group or collective identity based on one's perception that he or she shares a common heritage with a particular racial group" (Chavez & Guido-DiBrito, 1999, p. 40).

Racial identity: "the ways that individuals view themselves in relation to their [racial] group." (Chavous, Bernat, Schmeelk Cone, Caldwell, Kohn Wood, & Zimmerman, 2003).

Racial trauma: "race-based stress . . . [that] refers to the events of danger related to real or perceived experience of racial discrimination" (Comas-Diaz, 2019).

Racism: "a belief that human groups can be validly grouped according to their biological traits and that these identifiable groups inherit certain mental, personality, and cultural characteristics that determine their behavior" (Banks, p. 359).

Racist: "one who is supporting a racist policy through their actions or inaction or expressing a racist idea" (Kendi, 2019, p. 13).

White normativity: "the often unconscious and invisible ideas and practices that make whiteness appear natural and right" (Ward, 2008, p. 563).

References

Abacioglu, C. S., Volman, M., & Fischer, A. H. (2019). Teachers' multicultural attitudes and perspective taking abilities as factors in culturally responsive teaching. *British Journal of Educational Psychology*.

Abuse, S. (2014). SAMHSA's concept of trauma and guidance for a trauma-informed approach.

Arnett Jensen, L. (2003). Coming of age in a multicultural world: Globalization and adolescent cultural identity formation. *Applied Developmental Science, 7*(3), 189-196.

Aspen Institute. (2018). Pursuing social and emotional development through a racial equity Lens: A Call to Action.

Ayers, W. (2004). Teaching toward freedom. Boston: Beacon Press.

Banks, J. A., & Banks, C. A. (1993). *Multicultural Education: Issues and perspectives* (2nd ed.). Massachusetts: Allyn and Bacon.

Boykin, A. W., & Noguera, P. (2011). *Creating the opportunity to learn: Moving from research to practice to close the achievement gap*. Ascd.

Brown, K. T., & Ostrove, J. M. (2013). What does it mean to be an ally?: The perception of allies from the perspective of people of color. *Journal of Applied Social Psychology, 43*(11), 2211-2222.

Carr, P. & Lund, D. (2009). Antiracist education. In E. F. Provenzo & J. P. Renaud (Eds.), Encyclopedia of the cultural and social foundations of education (pp.48-52). Thousand Oaks, CA: Sage.

CASEL. (2020). Core SEL competencies. https://casel.org/core-competencies/

Chavez, A. F., & Guido-DiBrito, F. (1999). Racial and ethnic identity and development. *New directions for adult and continuing education, 84*, 39-47.

Chavous, T. M., Bernat, D. H., Schmeelk Cone, K., Caldwell, C. H., Kohn Wood, L., & Zimmerman, M. A. (2003). Racial identity and academic attainment among African American adolescents. *Child development, 74*(4), 1076-1090.

Chen, C. W., & Gorski, P. C. (2015). Burnout in social justice and human rights activists: Symptoms, causes and implications. *Journal of Human Rights Practice, 7*(3), 366-390.

Comas-Díaz, L., Hall, G. N., & Neville, H. A. (2019). Racial trauma: Theory, research, and healing: Introduction to the special issue. *American Psychologist, 74*(1), 1.

Cox, L. 2011. How Do We Keep Going? Activist Burnout and Sustainability in Social Movements. Helsinki: Into-ebooks

Diller, J. V. (2013). *Cultural diversity: A primer for the human services.* Nelson Education.

Dudley-Marling, C. (2015). The resilience of deficit thinking. *Journal of Teaching and Learning, 10*(1).

Engestrom, Y. (2000). Activity theory as a framework for analyzing and redesigning work.*Ergonomics, 43*(7), 960-974.

Engeström, Y. (2001). Expansive learning at work: Toward an activity theoretical reconceptualization. *Journal of education and work, 14*(1), 133-156.

Escayg, K. A. (2018). The missing links: Enhancing anti-bias education with anti-racist education. *Journal of Curriculum, Teaching, Learning and Leadership in Education, 3*(1), 15.

Farmer, R. F., & Chapman, A. L. (2016). *Behavioral interventions in cognitive behavior therapy: Practical guidance for putting theory into action.* American Psychological Association.

Fredricks, J. A., Blumenfeld, P. C., & Paris, A. H. (2004). School engagement: Potential of the concept, state of the evidence. *Review of educational research, 74*(1), 59-109.

Freudenberger, H.J. (1974) Staff burnout. Journal of Social Issues, 30, 159-165. doi:10.1111/j.1540-4560.1974.tb00706.x

Gay, G. (2018). *Culturally responsive teaching: Theory, research, and practice.* Teachers College Press.

Gedera, D. S. (2016). The application of activity theory in identifying contradictions in a university blended learning course. In *Activity theory in education* (pp. 51-69). Brill Sense.

Gee, J. P. (2018). Affinity spaces: How young people live and learn on line and out of school. *Phi Delta Kappan, 99*(6), 8-13.

Gillborn, D. (2006). Critical race theory and education: Racism and anti-racism in educational theory and praxis. *Discourse: studies in the cultural politics of education, 27*(1), 11-32.

Gorski, P. C. (2019). Fighting racism, battling burnout: Causes of activist burnout in US racial justice activists. *Ethnic and Racial Studies, 42*(5), 667-687.

Gorski, P. C., & Erakat, N. (2019). Racism, whiteness, and burnout in antiracism movements: How white racial justice activists elevate burnout in racial justice activists of color in the United States. *Ethnicities, 19*(5), 784-808.

Gould, S. J. (1996). *The mismeasure of man.* N.p.: W. W. Norton & Company.

Greene, G. (2018). *A burnt-out case.* Open Road Media.

Gretschel, P., Ramugondo, E. L., & Galvaan, R. (2015). An introduction to cultural historical activity theory as a theoretical lens for understanding how occupational therapists design interventions for persons living in low-income conditions in South Africa. *South African Journal of Occupational Therapy, 45*(1), 51-55.

Heyd, D. (2007). Justice and solidarity: The contractarian case against global justice. *Journal of Social Philosophy, 38*(1), 112-130.

Hollie, S. (2019). branding culturally relevant teaching: A Call for Remixes. *Teacher Education Quarterly, 46*(4), 31-52.

Imenda, S. (2014). Is there a conceptual difference between theoretical and conceptual frameworks? *Journal of Social Sciences, 38*(2), 185-195.

Inquiry, Stephen Lawrence. "Report of an inquiry by sir William MacPherson of Cluny." *TSO (The Stationery Office)* (1999).

Ismail, S. (2015). *Equity and Education. International Encyclopedia of the Social & Behavioral Sciences, 7*(2).

Jameson, D. A. (2007). Reconceptualizing cultural identity and its role in intercultural business communication. *The Journal of Business Communication (1973), 44*(3), 199-235.

Kendi, I. X. (2019). *How to be an antiracist.* One world.

Ladson illings, G. (1995). *But that's just good teaching! The case for culturally relevant pedagogy. Theory into practice, 34*(3), 159-165.

Ladson Billings, G. (2006). It's not the culture of poverty, it's the poverty of culture: The problem with teacher education. *Anthropology & Education Quarterly, 37*(2), 104-109.

Ladson-Billings, G. (2014). Culturally relevant pedagogy 2.0: aka the remix. *Harvard Educational Review, 84*(1), 74-84.

Laitinen, A., & Pessi, A. B. (2014). Solidarity: Theory and practice. An introduction. *Solidarity: Theory and practice*, 1-29.

Lund, D. E., & Carr, P. R. (Eds.). (2008). *Doing democracy: Striving for political literacy and social justice* (Vol. 322). Peter Lang.

Marshfield Clinic Division of Education (2020). Self-care plans: What and why? https://www.marshfieldclinic.org/education/residents-and-fellows/well-being-committee/well-being-topics/quality-of-life/self-care-plans-what-and-why

Merriam-Webster. (2020). Racism. In Merriam-Webster.com dictionary. Retrieved August 1, 2020, from https://www.merriam-webster.com/dictionary/racism

Noushad, P. P. (2008). *From teacher burnout to student burnout*. ERIC Clearinghouse.

NRDC (2019). Equity, Inclusion, Equality and Related Terms. https://www.broward.org/Climate/Documents/EquityHandout_082019.pdf

Omisakin, F. D., & Ncama, B. P. (2011). Self, self-care and self-management concepts: implications for self-management education. *Educational Research, 2*(12), 1733-1737.

Paris, D. (2012). Culturally sustaining pedagogy: A needed change in stance, terminology, and practice. *Educational researcher, 41*(3), 93-97.

Paris, D., & Alim, H. S. (Eds.). (2017). *Culturally sustaining pedagogies: Teaching and learning for justice in a changing world.* Teachers College Press.

Pines, A. (1994). Burnout in political activism: An existential perspective. *Journal of Health and Human Resources Administration, 164,* 381–394.

Ryan, W. (1971). *Blaming the victim.* New York, NY: Vintage.

Rychly, L., & Graves, E. (2012). Teacher characteristics for culturally responsive pedagogy. *Multicultural Perspectives, 14*(1), 44-49.

Samuels, A. J. (2018). Exploring culturally responsive pedagogy: Teachers' perspectives on fostering equitable and inclusive classrooms. *SRATE Journal*, *27*(1), 22-30.

Samuels, A. J., Samuels, G. L., & Cook, T. M. (2017). Examining perceptions of culturally responsive pedagogy in teacher preparation and teacher leadership candidates. *SRATE Journal*, *26*(2), 50-60.

Schaufeli, W., & Buunk, B. (2002). Burnout: An overview of 25 years of research and theorizing. In M. Schabracq, J. Winnubst, & C. Cooper (Eds.), *The handbook of work and health psychology* (pp. 383–425). Hoboken, NJ: Wiley.

Sivanandan, A. (2000). Reclaiming the struggle—One year on, Multicultural Teaching, 18 (2): 6-8 & 20.

Thrive Global (2018). 53 Self-care ideas for physical, emotional, and mental health https://thriveglobal.com/stories/self-care-ideas-for-physical-emotional-mental-health/

SAMHSA (2014). SAMHSA's concept of trauma and guidance for a trauma-informed approach. https://ncsacw.samhsa.gov/userfiles/files/SAMHSA_Trauma.pdf

Waitoller, F. R., & Kozleski, E. B. (2013). *Working in boundary practices: Identity development and learning in partnerships for inclusive education*. Teaching and Teacher Education, 31, 35-45.

Ward, J. (2008). White normativity: The cultural dimensions of whiteness in a racially diverse LGBT organization. *Sociological Perspectives*, *51*(3), 563-586.

Wenger, E. (2009). Communities of practice. *Communities*, *22*(5).

Wijeyesinghe, C. L., Griffin, P., & Love, B. (1997). Racism curriculum design. *Teaching for diversity and social justice: A sourcebook*, 82-109.

Williams, C. (1999). Connecting anti-racist and anti-oppressive theory and practice: retrenchment or reappraisal. *The British Journal of Social Work*, *29*(2), 211-230.

Woodson, C. G. (2006). The mis-education of the Negro. Trenton, NJ: Africa World Press

Books and Resources at Begin with Their Culture's Bookstore

Like Music to My Ears Curriculum
ISBN: 978-0-9847157-5-6

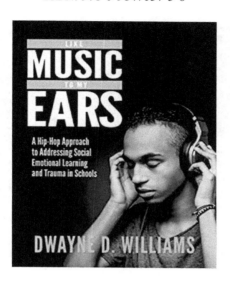

An RTI Guide to Improving Performance of African American Students
ISBN: 978-1483319735

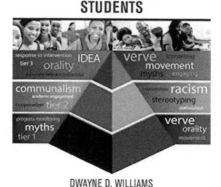

CPSIA information can be obtained
at www.ICGtesting.com
Printed in the USA
BVHW041305040621
608830BV00012B/283

9 780984 715725